A pacePILOT™ Guide

SAILING THROUGH Six SIGMA

How the Power of People Can Perfect Processes and Drive Down Costs

By
Michael Brassard and Diane Ritter

By the authors of **The Memory Jogger™** Series of Pocket Guides

In partnership with **Kent Sterett** and the **Premier Performance Network**

Intro

Ready ?

6 Months

Project

Long Haul

DMAIIC

Tools

R & R

*A pace*PILOT™ Guide:

Sailing Through Six Sigma
How the Power of People Can Perfect Processes and Drive Down Costs

Please respect ours, and other's, copyright

Software Design	George F. Brais, Brassard & Ritter, LLC
Graphics	Lori Champney, Manchester, NH
Copy Edit	Charles Terry, Stratham, NH
Six Sigma Black Belt	Materials provided and copyrighted by Premier Performance Network, York, PA and its members
Case Example	written by Paul Brassard, Cape Elizabeth, ME
Printing	Capital Offset Company Inc., Concord, NH

*pace*PILOT™ is a trademark of Brassard & Ritter, LLC
Post-It® *Notes* is a registered trademark of 3M Company
The Memory Jogger™ is a trademark of GOAL/QPC
Six Sigma® is a registered trademark of Motorola Co.
Champion℠, Black Belt℠, Green Belt℠, and Breakthrough Strategy℠ are service marks of Sigma Consultants, LLC

Questions, need info or help? Contact us.

Brassard & Ritter, LLC
P. O. Box 804
Marietta, GA
30061-0804

Phone: (770) 425-0375
Fax: (770) 425-0543
E-mail: info@pacepilot.com
Website: www. pacepilot.com
Toll Free: (888) 303-8669

ISBN: 0-9706839-0-1
Printed in the United States of America
First Edition
10 9 8 7 6 5 4 3 2 1

Our Thanks

To everyone who has supported us through this exciting project. We especially would like to thank:

OUR COLLEAGUES...

Premier Performance Network (PPN) for use of their Six Sigma Black Belt materials, advice, and guidance:

Boudewijn Bertsch	Mike Kelly	Ed Rhew
Mike Braid	Bill Marcacci	Kent Sterett
Brendan Collins	John O'Neill	Bob Wernley
William Henslcr		

Others who have so generously contributed advice, information, examples, or illustrations:

Mary Beavers, PPN, PA
Robert Mott, PPN, PA
Dianne Moulton, New Hampshire Ball Bearing, NH
Kevin Parker, Genesis Consulting, UK, a PPN partner
Alan Pelletier, New Hampshire Ball Bearing, NH
Ronald Snee, Snee Associates, DE
Jim St. Pierre, New Hampshire Ball Bearing, NH
Ed Zunich, Terrier Corporation, OH, a PPN partner

OUR FRIENDS AND SUPPORTERS...

Gloria & Paul Ackroyd	Lisa & Stephen Kuroski
Paul Brassard	Diana & Kent Sterett
Lori Champney	Doug Wike

OUR FAMILY...

Spouses Jaye, Paul, Betty; three of the very best
Illustrious Paige, Lauren, & Sarah
Xtraordinary Chris, Nina, Karin, Liz, & Mike

We might have missed some:

Soccer, baseball and softball practices or games
Incredible times together
Gymnastics, orienteering & swim practices or meets
Music and dance lessons or recitals
Agonizing homework assignments

Know that we love you for your patience and support throughout this extraordinary project!

Michael Brassard, Diane Ritter, and George Brais

A great network of friends and colleagues!

Intro

Ready?

6 Months

Project

Long Haul

DMAIIC

Tools

R & R

Intro

Ready ?

6 Months

Project

Long Haul

DMAIIC

Tools

R & R

About This Book

Sailing Through Six Sigma gives any manager immersed in the Six Sigma process what he or she needs to deal both with the "Art" (implementation issues) AND the "Science" (technical issues: the tools, techniques, processes, and calculations) of Six Sigma. How can we do justice to both dimensions in just 200+ pages? Enter the *pace*PILOT™ book with its companion CD-ROM and website.

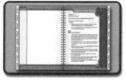

THE BOOK: The book gives you the high level summary that's portable: take it to class, management meetings or team problem-solving sessions.

THE E-BOOK/CD: Access the book on your computer! The CD is there to support you further, taking you as deep or as broad as your situation requires. Click any of the icons and get additional pop-up windows filled with more content, article

excerpts, and advice. This includes over 400 pages of the most up-to-date information available on Six Sigma systems and techniques. In addition, the e-book allows the reader to personalize the book by adding personal notes via text or audio, bookmarks, web links and attached files.

THE WEBSITE: Become a licensed member and link your e-book to our website which will provide access to over 1000 pages of even deeper Black Belt-level materials. This represents the most complete Six Sigma body of knowledge available on the market today. It's been built over the last 20 years and is still growing. With the low-cost *pace*PILOT™ license, this evolving material can be easily downloaded along with updates to the book, additional articles, case examples, new links and developments in Six Sigma technology. This allows *Sailing Through Six Sigma* to keep pace

www.pacePILOT.com

with the rapid learning curve in the field and your personal knowledge needs and learning style. The result of all of these features is a dynamic product that supports your daily journey to Six Sigma performance.

Navigating This Unique Book

No matter which media you use–book, e-book or website–we have organized it to help you quickly find the information you need:

✻ Begin with the table of contents or index in the book, or browse the Find Function in the e-book, to get a feel for the overall content.

✻ Or, just go to the first page of a particular colored tab in the book or click on the appropriate tab in the e-book to jump to a specific chapter.

✻ **Chapter Sections:** Throughout the chapters of the book and e-book you'll find several of the following sections.

- In Chapters 1-5, use the icons to visually and quickly find the start of each section.

    Purpose of this chapter: Get an overview of what's covered with specific highlights for senior executives and managers.

     The Big Picture: It's important to see the big picture to understand why and how key elements fit together, what the key activities, timing, and major milestones are.

     Expert Advice: Find the lessons learned and the warnings to heed based upon the experience of a network of executives, managers, and consultants who have successfully implemented Six Sigma and other organization-wide improvement programs.

     Spillover Lessons: Sometimes a book just isn't large enough to include everything you'd like to share. Click on the icon in the sidebar of the e-book next to the lessons or warnings for which you'd like more information.

     The Checklist: Things to make sure you've done or considered before moving on to the next phase of your implementation or problem-solving effort.

- In Chapter 6 you'll find the purpose of each sub-step within the steps of the DMAIIC problem-solving model, a quick reference listing of the necessary and sufficient tools (click on any tool in the e-book to find information about that tool) for that sub-step and a checklist of reminders of things to think about or do before moving on to the next sub-step.

Intro

Ready ?

6 Months

Project

Long Haul

DMAIIC

Tools

R & R

- In Chapter 7 you'll find the purpose, construction steps and a checklist of reminders for a few of the most important tools you and your team will use on a Six Sigma project team. You'll also see a comprehensive list of 100+ tools, methods, and theory that are only a click away from learning more about them.

✳ **Clickable Actions:** Whether book, e-book, or website, you'll also find:

- Underlined word(s): You see them in the book; go to the e-book and click on the underlined word(s) to enter "The PILOT" which will take you to basic or advanced (licensed Black Belt-type) content. After the first occurrence of underlining, simply pass your cursor over text and, if it changes to a hand, click on it to again link to The PILOT.

- Icons in the left- and right-sidebars. Click on these in the e-book to find the following types of pop-up windows:

 Idea: More information, excerpts from articles, additional lessons and warnings, etc.

 Chart: Find examples of tools, storyboards, forms, etc.

 Speaker: A short audio or video presentation from experts on specific topic areas.

 Slides: Pick up some how-to's, hints, and techniques in these short slide presentations.

✳ **The PILOT:** We couldn't fit everything in the book and keep it to a manageable size. So, additional information is *submerged* below and The PILOT is the navigational device that will steer you through it. When you click on a word or concept in the e-book, the PILOT will bring you to more information about it:

- Definitions
- Theory behind concepts and tools
- Examples
- Additional resources and links

So, *cast off* and *sail on* to learn more about Six Sigma...

Intro

Ready?

6 Months

Project

Long Haul

DMAIC

Tools

R & R

Table of Contents

Intro

Ready ?

6 Months

Project

Long Haul

DMAIIC

Tools

R & R

Intro

Ready ?

6 Months

Project

Long Haul

DMAIIc

Tools

R & R

Chapter 1:
Introduction to Six Sigma

The "business case," goals and components of a
Six Sigma management system.

Purpose of this chapter:

To provide the practical details of committing to a Six Sigma management system. It will answer the *who, what, where, when, why, and how much* questions of Six Sigma. The *how* of Six Sigma is the subject of the rest of the book.

For senior executives this chapter...
- Provides the general "business case" for Six Sigma.
- Provides a "typical" Six Sigma implementation process and timetable.

For managers at all levels this chapter...
- Serves as an outline for sharing the basics of Six Sigma with those reporting to you.
- Provides you with information that can help you convince people that Six Sigma is the wave of the future in successful businesses.
- Creates a clear picture of both the short-and long-term plan for implementing Six Sigma.

The Big Picture:

What is Six Sigma?

"Six Sigma is about creating a culture that demands perfection ... and that gives employees the tools to enable them to pinpoint performance gaps and make the necessary improvements ..."

Dow Chemical 2000 Annual Mtg. William S. Stavropoulos, Dow's president and CEO

"Six Sigma is a disciplined methodology, led and taught by highly trained GE employees... that focuses on moving every process that touches our customers - every product and service - toward near-perfect quality."

Jack Welch, Chairman and CEO, GE, Annual letter to share-owners in 1997.

Intro

Ready ?

6 Months

Project

Long Haul

DMAIC

Tools

R & R

Intro

Ready ?

6 Months

Project

Long Haul

DMAIIC

Tools

R & R

Chad Holliday,
Chairman and
CEO, DuPont
Sanford-
Bernstein
Conference, NYC,
6/8/00

Dan Burnham,
Chairman & CEO,
The Raytheon
Co. speaking to
Securities
Analysts 1/25/01

"Productivity is the third driver and offers enormous opportunity for DuPont. We've adopted Six Sigma methodologies as our process to unlock this value… projects include both cost reduction and incremental capacity improvement. Over time they'll have greater focus on revenue generation."

"Cash generation was a highlight for us. We generated a positive operating cash flow of $527 million in 2000, compared with $849 million in negative cash flow during 1999. It's been critical to us taking time out of the (business) cycle, which does indeed generate cash. Six Sigma generated an estimated $110 million in operating profit during 2000…We now have about 350 'experts' - some people have called them 'black belts'.

Based on the words of these seasoned executives, Six Sigma has three different, but related, meanings:

- Six Sigma is a **maniacal mindset** designed to get an entire organization focused on, and dedicated to, producing nearly perfect products and services that delight customers and realize higher profits.

- Six Sigma is a standard problem-solving **methodology** that can be applied to any process to eliminate the root cause of defects and associated costs (the DMAIIC model). It also features a methodology for designing new processes that better serve customer needs and generate new revenues (the DFSS/DMEDVI model).

- 6σ is a **measurement** that represents a company-wide performance goal of 3.4 defects per million opportunities for each product or service delivered.

> **At its simplest, Six Sigma is:**
> *A program to accelerate profits and customer satisfaction by systematically eliminating the root cause of critical defects/errors in all processes, or by creating new, more effective processes.*

Who's using Six Sigma as a key part of their competitive strategy?

Six Sigma is in use in virtually all industries around the world. In the U.S., 85 out of the Fortune 500 companies have programs underway. This figure doesn't include the countless smaller suppliers who have adopted Six Sigma in order to keep pace with these "Six Sigma Companies." The following is a very partial, but diverse list of Six Sigma companies:

- ABB (Asea Brown Bovari)
- Allied Signal/ Honeywell
- American Express
- Bombadier
- Citibank
- Dupont
- Dow Chemical
- Ericsson
- Ford Motor Co.
- General Electric
- Motorola
- Raytheon
- Sony

It's important to note that not all of these companies refer to their programs as "Six Sigma." They have most or all of the components of Six Sigma in place, but use program names like *Business Excellence*, *Premier Performance,* and *Six Sigma Plus*.

What kind of business results have some of these companies produced?

- During 1996 and 1997 *Allied Signal* recorded savings of $3.2 billion through their *Premier Performance* initiative.
- *Dow Chemical* projects a cumulative $1.5 billion of EBIT (operating income) from its launch in 1999 through 2003.
- *General Electric's* total Six Sigma benefit is expected to reach $5 billion by 2003.
- In 1999, *Honeywell* realized more than $600 million in *Six Sigma Plus*-related savings. The company expects year 2000 *Six Sigma Plus* cost savings to total $700 million.

Intro

Ready ?

6 Months

Project

Long Haul

DMAIC

Tools

R & R

What are the Core Principles of Six Sigma?

- Focus on **customer** satisfaction.
- Improve **profit** through increased revenue and reduced costs.
- Improve performance **project-by-project**.
- **Prioritize:**
  - *projects* based on their **impact on the business**
  - *defects/errors* based on **what matters most to the customer** AND their **impact on** the **cost** structure of the product or service.
- Manage the organization as a system of **connected processes**.
- Apply the Scientific Approach – Plan-Do-Check-Act (**PDCA**).
- Pursue **near perfection**.
- Use the full range of **statistical tools** that are available for analyzing and solving problems.
- **Respect** and build upon the knowledge, experience and dedication of **people** throughout the organization.

Words to Improve by...

Sigma (σ) – A Greek letter; it's a measure of the variation around the average of any process. Also known as 1 standard deviation, 1σ represents 34.134% of your data points.

6σ – A process quality measure indicating that there are 6 standard deviations between the process average and EACH (lower & upper) specification limit. Therefore, the greater the number of σ's, the smaller the variation (the tighter the distribution) around the average. If a process has 6σ's on each side of the average, it will produce approximately 3.4 <u>D</u>efects <u>P</u>er <u>M</u>illion <u>O</u>pportunities (see the following page for the DPMO Definition).

More Words to Improve by...

Master Black Belt – A full time person who's responsible for teaching, mentoring and reviewing Black Belts as well as for managing large-scale improvement projects.

Black Belt – A full time person intensively trained in quality management systems and advanced statistical tools and methods. He or she is assigned to work on critical business problems/opportunities alone or with teams.

Green Belt – A manager trained to work in support of Six Sigma initiatives on a part-time basis. They generally work part time as project team leaders on problems/opportunities that are smaller in scale than Black Belt projects.

Critical to Quality *(CTQ)* – What you manage and measure in the process that has a direct effect on the performance (or perceived performance) of the product or service in the hands of the customer.

DMAIIC *(Define, Measure, Analyze, Improve, Implement, Control)* – The standard steps for improving an existing process to a Six Sigma level.

DFSS *(Design For Six Sigma/DMEDVI: Define, Measure, Explore, Design, Validate, Implement)*
– A standard method for designing a new product or process capable of delivering Six Sigma level quality.

DPMO *(Defects Per Million Opportunities)* – Every product or service has 'x' number of CTQ's or "Opportunities for Defects." DPMO is the measure of the AVERAGE number of defects across ALL CTQ's that the current process will produce if not improved. Therefore, an automotive supplier with a 6σ process will NOT produce 3.4 defective transmissions per million. Rather, each transmission would have an average of 3.4 defects per million opportunities.

Intro

Ready ?

6 Months

Project

Long Haul

DMAIIC

Tools

R & R

Intro

Ready ?

6 Months

Project

Long Haul

DMAIIC

Tools

R & R

Even More Words to Improve by...

Hidden Factory – All of the in-process rework and/or repair activities created to turn defective product or services into 1st quality outputs. (SEE COPQ – Cost of Poor Quality)

Yield – The basic metric of process quality that measures the proportion of 1st quality product or service produced. There are four main types of yield measurements (you need to know AT LEAST the Final Yield and the Throughput Yield to even estimate the current 6σ level of a process):

FINAL YIELD – The proportion of products or service outputs that pass final inspection. It ignores the "hidden factory."

THROUGHPUT YIELD – The probability of any product or service passing through a particular process step without a defect or error.

ROLLED THROUGHPUT YIELD – The probability of any product or service passing through ALL of the process steps without a defect or error.

NORMALIZED YIELD – Based upon the Rolled Throughput Yield and the number of process steps, Normalized Yield creates an average yield for each step. This allows you to compare the yields of both simple (a few steps) and complex processes (many steps).

How is it different from past improvement efforts?

Since 1931, over 60 models (and countless company variations) have been developed by consultants and associations to improve quality, profitability, productivity, and cycle time. So, what's different? What is it about Six Sigma that's having such a profound effect on many of our leading corporations? None of the items in the following "Top 10" list should be considered in isolation since it's the **integration** of these differences that's so powerful, BUT... some are mentioned by Six Sigma veterans far more often than others.

A Six Sigma Program first and foremost...

1. **Intensively assigns and trains improvement experts** (Black Belts and Green Belts) to support and accelerate progress in every project. It's noteworthy that a significant percentage of candidates come from outside traditional "improvement training grounds" (e.g., Quality Assurance, Process and Industrial Engineering, etc.).

2. Tackles only those projects that have a significant impact on the **financials** of the organization.

3. Selects projects based upon their direct connection and contribution to the **strategic plan** of the organization.

A Six Sigma Program also...

4. Creates a singular **passion for dramatic and lasting improvement** that's infectious.

5. Requires the use of the full range of available **statistical tools** that can help to target and eliminate deeper root causes.

6. Addresses the highest **priority needs** of ALL of the **stakeholders** of any organization.

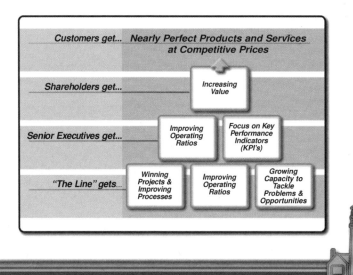

Intro

Ready ?

6 Months

Project

Long Haul

DMAIIC

Tools

R & R

7. Provides a single measure that can be used to **compare the performance** of very **different operations**. Prevents the traditional "you can't compare apples and oranges" argument.

    From the May 1, 2000 *Fortune* article, "The Odd Couple" – a conversation with Jack Welch (GE) and Scott McNealy (Sun Microsystems)...

    > **McNealy:** *What I'm finding in a company of 37,000 employees is that there are different dialects being created across the company, which makes it* hard *to get common reporting. You can't compare one organization with another. We have a saying inside Sun, 'If you can't measure it, you can't fix it.' You certainly can't measure it if you can't come up with the same labels for the axes of the charts and graphs. One of the advantages of getting a program going like this is that you get a common language.*

    > **Welch:** *That turned out to be true for us. When we go to Thailand and review a business, they're talking the same language because they're talking Six Sigma.*"

8. **Accelerates** the pace of **improvement** by using aggressive schedules, dedicated teams and projects led or guided by full-time "experts."

9. Pushes processes to produce **higher quality levels** than ever thought possible.

Most processes perform at a 3 to 4 Sigma level...

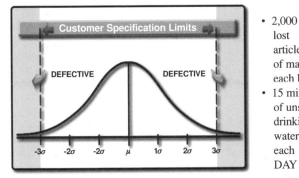

- 2,000 lost articles of mail each hour
- 15 minutes of unsafe drinking water each DAY

A Six Sigma process...

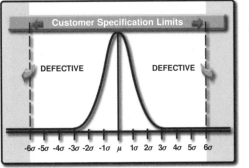

- 1 lost article of mail each hour
- 3 minutes of unsafe drinking water each YEAR!

6σ isn't twice as good as 3σ. It's almost 20,000 times better!

10. It's a **permanent program of project-by project improvement**, NOT an ill-defined journey. Six Sigma is proven, prescriptive and powerful. While it can be customized, Six Sigma seems to work best when it's mandated from the senior-leadership team and implemented aggressively with only minimal changes.

Ready ?   6 Months   Project   Long Haul   DMAIC   Tools   R & R

Ready?

6 Months

Project

Long Haul

DMAIIC

Tools

R & R

The Six Sigma Difference...

Profile of a Black Belt

This is a profile of Jim Fernandez. It's not meant to be a portrait of the perfect Black Belt. It's just Jim's story and his view of what's worked for him.

Background

In two high-tech manufacturers, Jim has been a Quality and Customer Satisfaction Manager for business units with up to $2 Billion in revenues. He has a technical Masters and an MBA.

What a Black Belt needs...

Jim doesn't put much stock in credentials. As a Black Belt he draws upon his experience as a *process thinker*. If hiring his replacement, he would first look for demonstrated ability to dramatically improve a variety of business processes. He would also look for a leader who's more interested in building a strong team than a strong resume.

What a Black Belt brings...

Jim is quick to point out that since every project is different, a good Black Belt senses the strengths and weaknesses of the team and adapts to fill the gaps. However, there are some roles that Jim feels that he needs to fill every time:

- Helping the team get to a clear consensus about the purpose of the project...and not allowing the team to move forward until it's there.
- Facilitating the team dynamics, especially since Six Sigma teams bring together people from different functions and processes.
- Choosing the right tool at the right time. In Jim's words, "Not trying to open a peanut with a sledgehammer."
- Getting the team to closure on the solution and plan, but NOT prematurely. He sees himself as guarding against "solutions in search of problems," and the tendency to interpret data to support a predetermined solution.

Signs of a Winning Project

Half kidding, Jim asked if he could answer "commitment, commitment, and commitment." He stressed that he looks for signs of commitment both from managers and the team members alike. Verbal commitment by the managers involved is necessary, but not sufficient to move ahead. Instead, he looks for two behaviors: commit the needed resources (don't skimp) and don't over-delegate. From the team members, Jim often uses a "change contract" to secure the two key behaviors: to participate (in body and spirit) and to follow through on assignments. Beyond commitment Jim looks for a well-defined problem statement and alignment from top to bottom on the priority of the problem (or opportunity).

A Favorite Project...

Jim's first project is his favorite, but not for sentimental reasons. It was not a typical first assignment. It was a problem affecting the entire company and creating a financial hemorrhage. Jim enjoyed the intensity and high visibility of the project, but he found even more satisfaction in bringing his 20 years of improvement experience to bear on a make-it-or-break-it business issue.

Another factor (and a wise move by the company) was the assignment of a second Black Belt to the project. Jim admits that Black Belt work can be a bit lonely at times and this "tag team" was stimulating and supportive.

What's Next?

Jim's company presents Black Belts with three career options:
1. Continue as a Black Belt in another part of the company.
2. Grow into a Master Black Belt.
3. Return to the operation as line manager or technical specialist (usually after 2-year Black Belt "hitches").

Jim is now moving towards his Master Black Belt certification. In fact, the mentoring role that is so central to being a Master Black Belt is fast becoming his favorite part of the job.

> *"It's become so gratifying on a day-to-day basis that some days I'm amazed that I'm paid to do it."*
> Jim Fernandez, Rochester, New York

Intro

Ready ?

6 Months

Project

Long Haul

DMAIIC

Tools

R & R

Intro
Ready ?
6 Months
Project
Long Haul
DMAIC
Tools
R & R

What does a typical implementation sequence and schedule look like?

Naturally, the length of time that it will take to implement a complete Six Sigma program will vary from company to company. The pace of implementation will be determined by factors such as:

- The size of the organization.
- The number of people who can be recruited and trained as Master Black Belts, Black Belts and Green Belts.
- The competitive "heat" being felt by the company.
- The financial resources that are available.
- The passionate commitment of top leadership.

Given these factors, the schedule below is a *typical* one for a mid-to-large size company.

Diagnose & Plan:	Months: 0-6
Introduce:	Months: 6-12
Expand:	Months: 12-24
Improve:	Months: 24+

Remember, the sequence and nature of the tasks DON'T change with each implementation. This is the proven path which:

- Develops a logical, systematic progression
- Builds internal skills quickly
- Obtains early quality and financial results
- Creates self-sustaining corporate momentum

- Clarify business strategies and identify performance gaps and opportunities.
- Decide that a Six Sigma program is the best response to these performance gaps and opportunities.
- Identify initial potential projects.
- Develop the implementation and resource plan.

Diagnose & Plan:
Months: 0 - 6

- Select or finalize first-round projects.
- Train senior managers and initial cadre of Black Belts, Green Belts, management sponsors and project team members.
- Demonstrate the power of Six Sigma through early wins and ROI.

Introduce:
Months: 6 - 12

Expand:
Months: 12 - 24

- More performance gaps addressed through Six Sigma.
- Focus on issues that impact customer loyalty. The revenue payback will be even faster and more dramatic than in the first-round projects.
- Stronger systems to support the work of "the Belts."
- Internal systems redesigned, starting with clear changes to the executive.

Intro

Ready ?

6 Months

Project

Long Haul

DMAIIC

Tools

R & R

Improve:
Months:
24 plus

- Increase the efficiency of Six Sigma projects.
- Wider application to new product/service design.*
- Regularly renew and reenergize.
- Wean the organization from external sources.

* This would be addressed in an earlier implementation phase (even in the Introduction Phase) if there are Critical-To-Quality (CTQ) issues in current products that are either visible at the time of purchase or that result in product failure within the first 3-6 months of ownership. Six Sigma methods should be applied as early as possible to such design issues because these issues can dramatically decrease customer loyalty, market share, short-term revenue and profitability while increasing company liability for producing known defects.

 ## Expert Advice:

Lesson #1 – *Introducing a major improvement program such as Six Sigma seems to work best when there's a "burning platform."*

A critically "hot issue" with important implications for the direction of the business is often referred to as a "burning platform." This should be the focal point for Six Sigma since an organization's culture often has to be "shocked" in order to change its direction and momentum. This type of focus will attract the attention and participation that Six Sigma needs if it's to play an important role in the company's future.

Following are some examples of the "burning platforms" used by leading Six Sigma companies.

Allied Signal – 1991:

When Larry Bossidy became the CEO of Allied Signal in 1991, it was a tired organization. Its more than 70,000 employees in 40 countries produced products for some of the most mature industries in the economy. Morale and returns to shareholders were falling. It was the type of company that was worth more broken into discrete businesses than continuing as a single enterprise. Bossidy used Six Sigma as the centerpiece of his plan to unite and rejuvenate the company.

Allied Signal "Burning Platform"	The Six Sigma Response
Low morale	Educated, empowered employees (40 hours per employee/year)
Average quality	Strive for perfection (99.4% error-free/4 Sigma level)
Marginal return-on-equity	Industry-leading earnings-per-share (3x improvement)
Marginally satisfied customers	Delighted customers
Margin squeeze	Exponential margin growth (2x improvement)
Stagnating productivity	Productivity explosion (6% annual increase)

Sun Microsystems – 1999:

In June 1999 eBay, the on-line auction house, lit the fuse for Sun Microsystems' "burning platform." A bug in a Sun server caused the eBay web site to go down for 22 hours. This was just the latest in a series of smaller server-related outages, but for Scott McNealy, Sun's CEO, this incident spotlighted the core competitive issue in the server market: RELIABILITY. As a result, Sun launched "Sun Sigma" as part of a massive corporate culture change process. The goal was simple: to make a Sun server as reliable (and expected)

Intro

Ready ?

6 Months

Project

Long Haul

DMAIC

Tools

R & R

as a phone's dial tone. The incentive for top managers was equally simple: lead a significant Sun Sigma project in the next 18 months or forego that next promotion.

Lesson #2 – *The ultimate measure of success is an IMPROVED BOTTOM LINE. Six Sigma projects help to achieve this by increasing revenue AND driving down cost, while meeting the needs and expectations of customers in your highest growth /profit markets.*

Many years ago Dr. Joseph Juran, one of the fathers of the "Improvement Revolution" said, "The key to making quality a priority is to translate it into the language of management, *money."* Even more strategically, Six Sigma must address problems and opportunities in areas that produce the *future profit*. It must be seen as a key to the competitive future of the organization AND not as a way to keep declining areas afloat.

Six Sigma Generates Revenue…

In Manufacturing and Service…
- By making products/services more reliable than those of competitors and therefore increasing sales.

- By reducing waste and defects in the processes, these more reliable products/services can then be sold at a lower price. This captures market share, while maintaining margins.

- By lowering prices or holding them constant (due to lower costs such as fewer defects), increasing sales (due to better reliability and more competitive pricing) and lowering costs (due to productivity gains) revenues and margins can be increased.

- By providing extraordinary value to, and integration with, customers and their processes. Customers become dependent and effectively can't (or don't want to) leave the relationship. This makes it possible to charge above-market prices while controlling costs.

In Education, Healthcare and Government…
- By reducing waste and rework in processes, more can then

be done with the declining budgeted dollars (or capped reimbursements in healthcare), thereby creating a "service profit." This could be in the form of a budget surplus, but it's more likely that it would allow services to reach more people in need.

• By increasing "shareholder" value by providing more effective services per tax or insurance-premium dollar.

Whether expressed as "profit" or "available funds," money IS the lifeblood of any organization. Six Sigma uses this bottom-line focus as a way to create a standard measure of success that is as meaningful to a CEO as it is to a line manager.

GE has taken this emphasis on profit even further. Through its "outside-in" approach to quality, GE plans to increasingly focus Six Sigma projects on improving its CUSTOMERS' profitability. This makes GE an even more valued supplier and Six Sigma an essential part of their relationship.

A final note… Six Sigma has also been used at the other end of the supply chain. Serious Six Sigma users are looking to improve their own profitability by requiring that its suppliers take cost out of purchased products and services using Six Sigma methods. They're looking at Six Sigma both as a way to deliver real price reductions and to eliminate suppliers who aren't dedicated to ongoing product and process improvement.

Intro

Ready ?

6 Months

Project

Long Haul

DMAIIC

Tools

R & R

The Six Sigma Difference...

What's The Impact of Your Current Sigma Level on Your Bottom Line?

The most compelling reason for pursuing Six Sigma is purely economic: processes operating at a 6σ level deliver products at a lower cost and/or higher revenue level. Cost categories like scrap, rework, and warrantee claims are directly reduced because the product or service meets customer specifications 99.99966% of the time. Other cost categories, such as loss of reputation, customer movement to competitors, and opportunity costs on capital now devoted to dealing with quality problems, are more difficult to quantify. On the other hand, revenue growth due to increased market share and premium pricing also flow from having 6σ processes in place.

Consider the following figures from Harry and Schroeder's, *Six Sigma: The Breakthrough Strategy Revolutionizing the World's Top Corporations* (Random House, NY, 2000):

Sigma Level	Cost of Poor Quality
2	Not Competitive
3	25-40% of gross sales
4	15-25% of gross sales
5	5-15% of gross sales
6	Less than 1% of gross sales

What current strategies do you have that would deliver this level of improvement in your balance sheet?

The Six Sigma Difference...

More on The Impact of Your Current Sigma Level on Your Bottom Line

To begin to see the size of the potential financial return on your investment in Six Sigma (See Chapter 3: The First 6 Months for typical implementation costs), first estimate the process Sigma level of one of your important products or services.

(Use the Six Sigma Estimator in the companion e-book.)

With just a few key points of data from your quality records, it will calculate the following measures for your sample process:

- The Final Yield
- The Defect Rate Per CTQ
- The Defects Per Million Opportunities (DPMO)

You can then calculate your Sigma performance on that one process and begin to project the financial impact based on the figures put forth by Harry and Schroeder. Remember that this is just a rough estimate as you begin to understand the size of your overall improvement opportunity.

Lesson #3 – *"Process execution" has never been more important.*
The margin for error in producing quality products and services has been getting smaller for over 20 years. The Japanese changed the competitive rules during the 70's and 80's. Western companies either responded to the challenge or got out of those businesses.

During the 90's technology became a key driver for change.

Technology:
- Decreased transaction times.
- Shortened the feedback loop between suppliers and customers.
- Made it possible to integrate data systems within and between companies.

Technology, in short, established a new pace that doesn't tolerate variation. At the same time, customers have become increasingly demanding. The job of management is to balance its own internal efforts, such as Just-in-Time delivery, Supply-Chain Management, etc. with the rising expectations of customers. In order to achieve this balance, processes have to be virtually perfect and predictable.

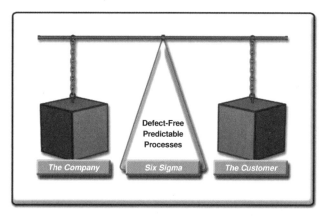

GE has been trying to achieve this balance since introducing its "Work-Out" program in the 80's. It was designed to "get rid of the dumb stuff" in all operations. Six Sigma built upon this foundation of concerted organization-wide improvement when it was introduced in the 90's.

The company's "e-Business" initiative is an ideal next step. It's a natural marriage with Six Sigma for three reasons:

1. The company realized from the beginning that "e-businesses" fail when the supporting processes are not at a Six Sigma level. This is a lesson that many of the dot com companies learned too late.

2. It uses Six Sigma to perfect "e-processes." This is even more essential than in manual processes, since there are no people involved who can "finesse" the process to make it work. This is the same principle that applied to the intro duction of robotics in manufacturing.

3. The "e-processes" are just plain faster and more accurate. This allows processes to reach even higher Sigma levels.

Honeywell has taken this marriage of Six Sigma and "e-processes" one step further. Its direct-purchasing web sites, *MyPlant.com*, *MyAircraft.com*, and *MyFacilities.com* came directly from Six Sigma Plus projects.

Lesson #4 – Six Sigma requires top management drive

> *"A company cannot buy its way into quality —*
> *it must be led into quality by top management."*
>
> Dr. W. Edwards Deming
> ***Out of the Crisis,*** 1986

Successful Six Sigma implementations have once again proved Dr. Deming to be correct. Although some Six Sigma programs have succeeded by "starting small," the most powerful examples have been driven from the top and implemented broadly.

Throughout the book, this leadership role will be highlighted in the different phases of implementation, but below is an overview of the major leadership responsibilities, broken down into three categories: *Values*, *Behaviors* and *System Changes*.

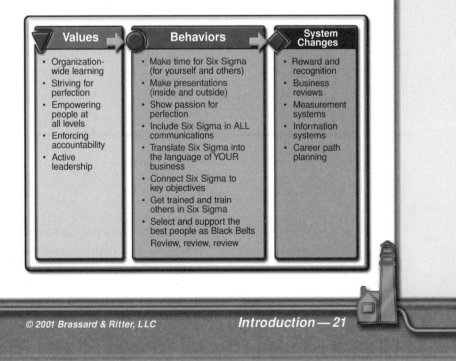

Values
- Organization-wide learning
- Striving for perfection
- Empowering people at all levels
- Enforcing accountability
- Active leadership

Behaviors
- Make time for Six Sigma (for yourself and others)
- Make presentations (inside and outside)
- Show passion for perfection
- Include Six Sigma in ALL communications
- Translate Six Sigma into the language of YOUR business
- Connect Six Sigma to key objectives
- Get trained and train others in Six Sigma
- Select and support the best people as Black Belts
- Review, review, review

System Changes
- Reward and recognition
- Business reviews
- Measurement systems
- Information systems
- Career path planning

A few examples of leadership in action:

Values

Larry Bossidy at Allied Signal budgeted 2% of the annual payroll to fund 40 hours of mandated education per employee per year.

Behavior

Patrick Donovan, CEO of BSS, a mid-sized heating equipment distributor in the UK, was told by his consultant that he should expect to spend about 20% of his time involved in the improvement process. After 6 months, he concluded that his consultant was wrong. He really needed to spend 100% of his time on the process, since creating a culture of dramatic improvement was his ENTIRE job as a leader.

 Executive Team...

You've been asked in the past to let major organizational changes "take root" in lower parts of the organization so that people could "own" the change. In contrast, the most successful Six Sigma leaders have:

1. Aggressively demanded management participation AND performance (not simply compliance).

2. Replaced those who wouldn't change with others who would.

These two actions will have more impact than any training, bonuses, competitive data, and examples you could ever provide.

System Changes

At *GE*, the executive bonus system, which applies to nearly 10,000 top managers, (Cash bonuses can increase as much as 150% in a year, to between 20% and 70% of base pay plus stock options) has become a major portion of the compensation system. As much as 40 percent of that bonus is now tied to Six Sigma implementation.

Lesson #5 – Black Belts need to be full-time, rather than part-time positions.

The availability of a cadre of highly trained Black Belts has turbo-charged the Six Sigma process. Since the Black Belts will be (and MUST be) some of the highest performers in the organization, there's a natural temptation to create a part-time schedule. This is a mistake for 4 reasons:

1. It's difficult for a part-time Black Belt to focus completely on his or her #1 job: to help move Six Sigma projects to a quick and successful completion.

2. The benchmarked return-on-investment for full-time Black Belts is so impressive, why change the formula? For example,

   - $150,000 - $175,000 savings/revenue enhancement per project

   - $500,000 - $1,000,000 contribution per year/per Black Belt

3. Creating *full*-time Black Belts is a **powerful** sign of the *full* commitment to the Six Sigma process by the leaders of the organization.

4. Since full-time Black Belts experience more projects, they continue to sharpen their skills and accelerate the pace of improvement even further.

Spillover Lessons…

Every book requires an author to make choices, usually between breadth and depth. This choice is even tougher in a small-format book. Enter the e-book… this provides the opportunity to highlight the most critical information in the text AND give the reader the option to see more.

In this section, the key lessons from Six Sigma experts are included in the book. Other important lessons are listed below. They are well worth reading, but they are on the other side of an admittedly arbitrary line. Once in the e-book, just click on the icon next to the Lesson # you want to view in its entirety.

Intro

Ready ?

6 Months

Project

Long Haul

DMAIIC

Tools

R & R

Lesson #6 – *Implementing Six Sigma is like frying small fish*

Lesson #7 – *Train, Do, Train, Do…*

✓ The Check List:

Have you…

- ❏ Evaluated your own business situation to see if there's a fit with Six Sigma?

- ❏ Begun to understand the major components of Six Sigma as a management philosophy, process measurement and improvement method?

- ❏ Built a general picture of the next 2-3 years, if you've decided to implement Six Sigma in your organization?

- ❏ Evaluated the impact of a Six Sigma program on your personal leadership style?

- ❏ Projected the positive impact of a Six Sigma program on the bottom line of your organization?

Intro

Ready ?

6 Months

Project

Long Haul

DMAIIC

Tools

R & R

Chapter 2:
Are You Ready?

Preparing to successfully launch your Six Sigma program

Purpose of this chapter

To provide an overview of what an organization must do to prepare for a successful Six Sigma implementation.

For senior executives this chapter...

- Provides an overview of the "necessary and sufficient" steps to both assess and prepare your organization for making Six Sigma a way of life.
- Provides a guide to the Six Sigma behaviors that you should adopt to support implementation.
- Puts Six Sigma into a "change management" context, rather than into a series of technical steps and tools.

For managers at all levels this chapter...

- Provides a glimpse into the planning process that precedes a typical Six Sigma program launch.
- Shows how you can support top leadership in making some of the necessary system changes.
- Specifies what you personally can do to ensure a successful Six Sigma implementation, since you are viewed as senior management in your part of the organization.

The Big Picture

What's the biggest leadership challenge?

In this diagnosis and planning phase, it's essential to first view Six Sigma as you would any major-change process in your organization. Remember that the overriding question that EVERYONE will ask is:

> *"Why should we do anything different at this time?"*

Intro

Ready ?

6 Months

Project

Long Haul

DMAIC

Tools

R & R

How thoughtfully you answer this question will largely determine whether Six Sigma is:

A fundamental shift in the culture and competitiveness of your organization.

or

Just another program that can be ignored since "it too shall pass."

It would be wonderful to say that there's a "science" to creating such a fundamental shift in the culture, but this is where the "art" of Six Sigma begins. Luckily, there are experienced Six Sigma "artisans" who have discovered some things that work. This chapter will share some of that experience.

What are the major tasks?

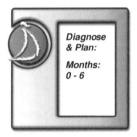

Diagnose & Plan:

Months: 0 - 6

- Clarify business strategies and identify performance gaps and opportunities.
- Decide that a Six Sigma program is the best response to these performance gaps and opportunities.
- Identify initial potential projects.
- Develop the implementation and resource plan.

This intensive six-month planning process is designed to produce one thing: *an aggressive, but achievable, Six Sigma implementation plan that's firmly rooted in the competitive realities of the business.* In order for people throughout the organization to commit to the hard work of living and breathing Six Sigma, it MUST be seen as a logical response to a serious problem.

Following is a <u>Responsibility Flow Chart</u> that breaks this planning process into more detail. Notice that the process involves different levels of the organization at different times. This reflects the experience of the most successful companies, which use a blend of "top-down" and "bottom-up" approaches.

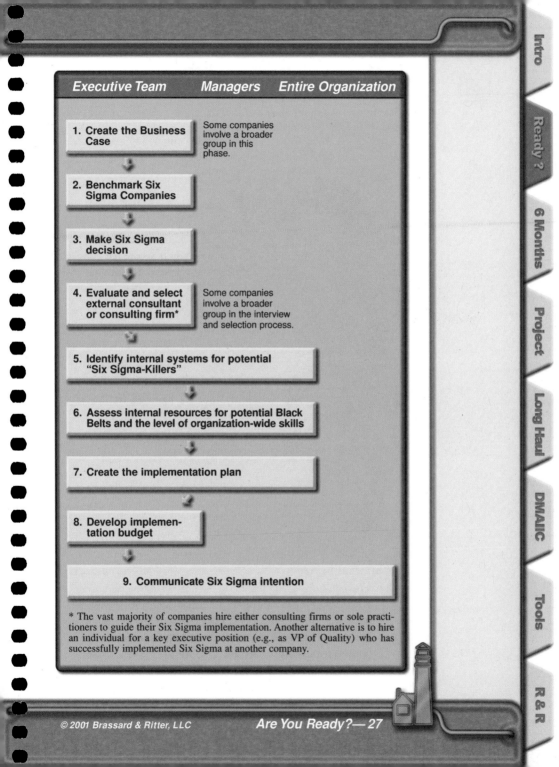

Executive Team · Managers · Entire Organization

1. **Create the Business Case** — Some companies involve a broader group in this phase.

2. **Benchmark Six Sigma Companies**

3. **Make Six Sigma decision**

4. **Evaluate and select external consultant or consulting firm*** — Some companies involve a broader group in the interview and selection process.

5. **Identify internal systems for potential "Six Sigma-Killers"**

6. **Assess internal resources for potential Black Belts and the level of organization-wide skills**

7. **Create the implementation plan**

8. **Develop implementation budget**

9. **Communicate Six Sigma intention**

* The vast majority of companies hire either consulting firms or sole practitioners to guide their Six Sigma implementation. Another alternative is to hire an individual for a key executive position (e.g., as VP of Quality) who has successfully implemented Six Sigma at another company.

Intro
Ready ?
6 Months
Project
Long Haul
DMAIC
Tools
R & R

1. Create the Business Case – *Executive Team (plus Managers in some cases)*

The Executive Team must start the Six Sigma planning process by connecting Six Sigma and the core of the business. It's their job to develop a *Business Case* that provides the compelling reasons for the organization to change. A business case includes both the forces that are making change necessary AND how a Six Sigma management system is an effective response to those forces.

The Business Case: Part One – *What's our strategy, given all of the forces for major change?*

Building the Business Case starts with a well-executed strategic planning process. The Executive Team should assess the current strategy in light of the competitive environment and internal strategic thinking.

a. Exploring the Forces for Change

The following are typical categories and questions to consider:

External Forces

Competitors–Are new or existing competitors capturing a growing share of the market based upon dramatically better product or service reliability and/or a significantly lower cost structure?

Financial Stakeholders–For public companies, are shareholders demanding vastly improved stock and/or dividend performance? For private companies, are financial institutions, including venture capitalists looking for higher return-on-asset performance?

Technology –Are there emerging technologies that are dramatically changing the cost structure and/or reliability of a major product or service line?

Internal Forces

Vision Shift –Is the leader, the senior executive team, or Board of Directors pushing the organization to change its basic direction or position in the market? For example, are key players suggesting a shift from a highly customized, premium-priced product line to a limited option, price-leader position?

Intro

Ready?

6 Months

Project

Long Haul

DMAIC

Tools

R & R

b. Setting the Strategy

Once it's decided which "signals" from the environment are most important, work hard to create an ABSOLUTELY CLEAR strategy statement that can serve as *the* direction setter for all decisions at any level of the organization. If you already have a strategy statement that serves this purpose, confirm that it includes the following components:

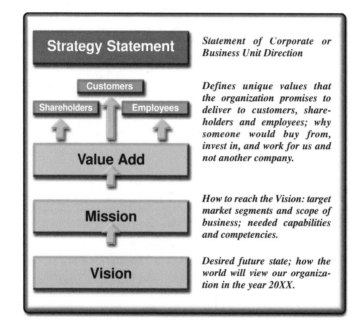

Strategy Statement — *Statement of Corporate or Business Unit Direction*

Customers
Shareholders / Employees

Value Add — *Defines unique values that the organization promises to deliver to customers, shareholders and employees; why someone would buy from, invest in, and work for us and not another company.*

Mission — *How to reach the Vision: target market segments and scope of business; needed capabilities and competencies.*

Vision — *Desired future state; how the world will view our organization in the year 20XX.*

c. Establishing the Business Growth Plan

This portion of the Business Case deals with the touchstone of Six Sigma: the financials. What are the financial targets that the strategy is designed to accomplish? Said another way, what are the financial measures of the strategy's success or failure?

This is a critical piece of making the decision to do Six Sigma because it quantifies how much improvement is enough to achieve the strategic direction.

Intro

Ready ?

6 Months

Project

Long Haul

DMAIC

Tools

R & R

Intro

Ready?

6 Months

Project

Long Haul

DMAIC

Tools

R & R

The following example is taken from the actual improvement plan of one of the major U.S. rail carriers. Below is the beginning of the rollout of one of its 5-year strategic plans. It clearly spelled out the size of the business challenge that lay ahead and was the first step toward identifying improvement projects.

Always Set an Overall Financial Target: Without one, it's impossible to judge the size/importance of the potential contribution of Six Sigma.

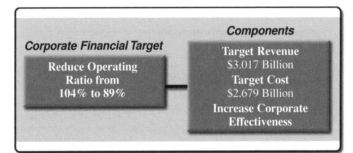

Corporate Financial Target

Reduce Operating Ratio from 104% to 89%

Components

Target Revenue
$3.017 Billion

Target Cost
$2.679 Billion

Increase Corporate Effectiveness

The Business Case: Part Two – *How does a Six Sigma management system begin to respond to these changes?*

Six Sigma serves as a management system because its improvement projects flow directly from the company or business unit strategy and financial goals. The next step is to break down the components above into more specific categories.

a. Identifying and Analyzing Performance Indicators

Based on the work of Kaplan and Norton in *The Balanced Scorecard, 1996,* Performance Indicators are the measures that provide a complete picture of the organizational health of your company. They are also the "bridge" between the company-wide growth goals and concrete improvement projects.

The standard Kaplan and Norton categories are listed below, along with questions that will allow you to select performance measures most relevant to your business:

Customer – how do customers see us (satisfaction, loyalty, brand image)?

Process – how well do we perform (productivity, speed, asset utilization, inventory turns)?

Innovation and Learning – can our people improve and

Intro
Ready ?
6 Months
Project
Long Haul
DMAIC
Tools
R & R

create value (recruiting, employee retention, innovation, teamwork, harnessing or creating new technology)?

Financial – how do we look to shareholders (profit, sales revenue, Return-On-Assets (ROA), Price/Earnings (PE) Ratio)?

The rail carrier next identified and measured Performance Indicators in all of the BSC categories related to *generating revenue, cutting costs or improving corporate effectiveness.* This created a master list of potential areas of improvement, along with their financial impact on either the revenue or cost side of the business. There can be as many as 100 Performance Indicators (PI's) in this master list.

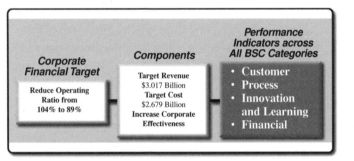

b. Identifying Focus Areas for Improvement

The final piece of the business case is the identification of focus areas from among all of your Performance Indicators. Below, our railroad carrier chose the Focus Areas as program "drivers":

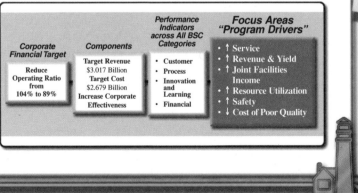

Choose carefully! Your focus areas will drive the entire Six Sigma program

Intro

Ready ?

6 Months

Project

Long Haul

DMAIIC

Tools

R & R

Choosing Focus
Areas is not just a
numbers game...the
areas selected must
be Measurable
AND Motivating!

Measurable

It's critical that each one of these Focus Areas has readily available data to measure and compare performance. Following are a few examples of indicators from the "Cost of Poor Quality" (COPQ) area:

- Locomotive Utilization
- Empty Car Movement

- Derailment
- Rejected Cars
- Premature Parts Failure

- Billing Errors & Disputes
- Train Delays

Doing a Pareto analysis of these indicators (and those in the other Focus Areas) will later surface Six Sigma projects.

Motivating

Each Focus Area MUST also represent a dramatic improvement opportunity. Otherwise, daily operations (and the inevitable emergencies) will always take precedence. If you were an executive or manager in our railroad carrier, would the Cost of Poor Quality figures in the following charts get and keep your attention?

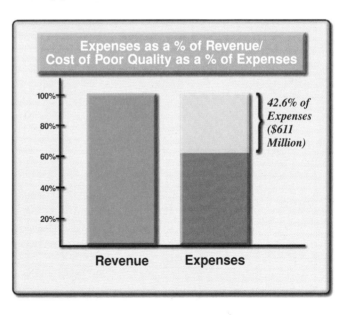

**Expenses as a % of Revenue/
Cost of Poor Quality as a % of Expenses**

42.6% of Expenses ($611 Million)

Revenue   Expenses

The Six Sigma Approach to Reducing Expenses

Across the Board % Cost Cut

Revenue   Traditional Approach

Cut Cost/Eliminate Waste

Necessary and productive Expenses, "The Engine"

Revenue   Six Sigma Approach

This example is motivating for two reasons. First, $611 million worth of improvement opportunities gives EVERYONE confidence that he or she can identify meaningful projects. Secondly, Six Sigma attacks the disease (waste), NOT the healthy, productive parts of the operation. Traditional "slash and burn" cost-cutting programs indiscriminately cut budgets and the spirits of good people at all levels of the organization.

Intro

Ready ?

6 Months

Project

Long Haul

DMAIC

Tools

R & R

2. **Benchmark Six Sigma companies –** *Executive Team*

There are some simple ways to learn from the growing list of companies that have committed to implementing Six Sigma:

- Arrange for on-site visits to Six Sigma customers, suppliers and non-competitors. There is no substitute for observing the process and results first hand.
- Review the rate of change in their key financial indicators of improvement, such as Return on Assets, PE Ratios and Market Share.
- Search the Web Sites of your competitors, suppliers and customers for Six Sigma references. It's a quick way both to get an overview of their efforts and to gauge the depth of their commitment.
- Regularly search the Web for news stories, articles and press releases using Six Sigma as a keyword.

3. **Make the Six Sigma decision –** *Executive Team*

- Step #1 (*Business Case*) proves to the senior executive team (and eventually the rest of the organization) that implementing Six Sigma is *necessary.*
- Step #2 (*Benchmarking*) then proves that it's *possible.*
- It's the job of the leadership team to turn this knowledge into a *commitment to doing whatever's needed* to make Six Sigma a reality over the long haul.

4. **Evaluate and select external consultant or consulting firm –** *Executive Team*

The choice of the person or consulting firm to guide Six Sigma implementation is one of the most important decisions that the Executive Team will make. All of the most successful implementations have used experienced external consultants who have saved those companies *months,* and even *years,* in their implementation process.

Their experience will help you choose *better targets* AND design the *most efficient path* to those targets.

Intro
Ready ?
6 Months
Project
Long Haul
DMAIIC
Tools
R & R

Consultant Selection Criteria	Consultant A	Consultant B	Consultant C
Line Management experience			
Senior Executive experience			
Quality Specialists with the experience in your industry			
Experience in multi-national corporations (must match your structure)			
Chemistry with Senior Executives			
Amount of Company-wide implementation experience			
Documented results			

5. **Identify internal systems for potential "Six Sigma killers" –** *Executive Team and Managers*

Accepting Myron Tribus's principle of "system ownership" is fundamental to moving a company to a Six Sigma system of management. Leaders should, therefore, work with managers "in the trenches" to review pieces of the management system that either under-perform or send contradictory messages to that of Six Sigma.

Pay special attention to the following systems (they are in order of priority):

- Reward and Recognition
- Operations Reviews
- Accountability
- Project Management
- Training and Education
- Information and Technology (IT)

"Management works ON the system, everyone else works IN the system." Myron Tribus, former Director of Advanced Engineering Studies at MIT

Intro

Ready?

6 Months

Project

Long Haul

DMAIC

Tools

R & R

Also identify where there is NO SYSTEM in place. Some would say that this is good news since you don't have to break bad habits; the bad news is that this situation often indicates a lack of organizational discipline and accountability. Building these two habits from scratch is usually a bigger challenge than redesigning a broken system.

You will see in this book and in many articles that serious Six Sigma companies have made a total commitment to aligning all of these systems. These changes have played a major role in making Six Sigma a permanent part of their management approach.

6. **Assess internal resources for potential Black Belts and the level of organization-wide skills** – *Executive Team and Managers*

One piece of the Six Sigma formula for success is pretty obvious:

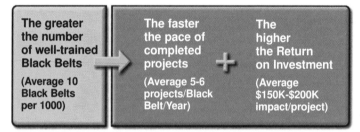

| The greater the number of well-trained Black Belts (Average 10 Black Belts per 1000) | → | The faster the pace of completed projects (Average 5-6 projects/Black Belt/Year) | + | The higher the Return on Investment (Average $150K-$200K impact/project) |

The ROI is obvious, but so is the size of the human resource commitment that's needed. At a minimum, your organization needs to identify and/or train:

- *Project managers* to coordinate complex projects. This allows Black Belts to support parallel projects. This is necessary if 5-6 projects are to be completed per year with projects typically lasting 4-6 months.
- *Champions* who ensure that projects are on track and fully supported.
- *Green Belt* candidates who can support the Black Belts in the major projects and act as team leaders for smaller-scale efforts.

- *Black Belt* candidates who fit this description found on the Motorola Six Sigma web page.

  Black Belts are…

  …Experienced professionals, often engineers

  …Change agents

  …Highly respected by their peers

  …Internal consultants to senior management

  …Able to transfer new Quality ideas, tools and strategies to business units

  …Mentors

  …Coaches

  …Able to Spread best practices and detect system problems

It's clear that finding and developing the right people to coordinate and lead Six Sigma projects is the #1 planning priority.

7. Create the implementation plan – *Executive Team and Managers*

This is an opportunity to achieve that elusive management commitment that's so critical in a major change program like Six Sigma. Expand the planning group beyond the executive team into an "Implementation Team" to build the "what" and the "how" of Six Sigma. This team usually includes the functional managers who show the most enthusiasm for the potential business impact of the process.

Deploying the Targets: *The What* – The <u>Deployment Tree Diagram</u> is a powerful planning and communications tool. It:

- Helps the planning team confirm that EVERY Six Sigma project is connected to the strategy.
- Also provides a snapshot of those connections to the entire organization.

Intro

Ready?

6 Months

Project

Long Haul

DMAIIC

Tools

R & R

Intro

Ready?

6 Months

Project

Long Haul

DMAIC

Tools

R & R

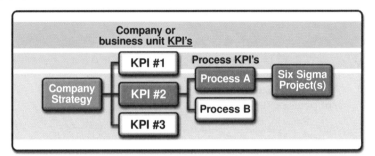

Deploying the Six Sigma Program: *The How* – This includes the practical details of how the Six Sigma program will take aim at the targets in the Deployment Tree Diagram above. See Lesson #3 later in this chapter for details about what this part of the implementation plan should include.

Develop the implementation budget – *Executive Team*
The most important feature of any budget is that it's REALISTIC in terms of:

- The amount of revenue/cost reduction that will be generated.
- The Six Sigma program implementations costs.

8. **Communicate Six Sigma intention** – *Entire Organization*

Every stakeholder of your organization has a strong interest in the success or failure of Six Sigma. However, use some caution and common sense when deciding what and when you communicate with each group. The following is the recommended order and content of those communications:

From the beginning…

1. Line managers & employees
    - How this will make their jobs easier.
    - How it will make their futures both more exciting and secure.
    - Their role in making it happen.
    - That this is NOT a voluntary process.
    - Any structural change.
    - Stronger emphasis on Review, Reward and Accountability.

RULE #1:
Communicate with each stakeholder group when the process is about to affect them.

RULE #2:
Provide information that specifies the impact of the process on them.

© 2001 Brassard & Ritter, LLC

When projects depend on incoming goods and services...

2. Suppliers
    - How it will change our relationship and performance expectations.

When there are significant examples and savings (not promises) to Showcase...

3. Shareholders
    - How it will increase the short- and long-term value of their holdings.
4. Customers
    - How it will affect the reliability and value of the products and services they buy.

 **Expert Advice:**

Lesson #1 – *Make sure that your strategic business plan is well known and understood by EVERYONE in the organization.*

If the benefits of sharing the strategic business plan are so great, then every company must be doing it, right? Wrong.

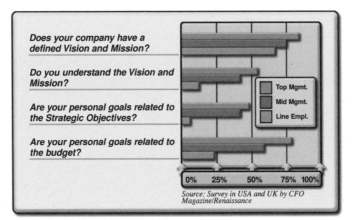

Source: Survey in USA and UK by CFO Magazine/Renaissance

Jack Welch, General Electric's legendary CEO, understands the power of a shared strategy. When he stated in the 90's "GE would be #1 or #2 in any of our businesses," people listened. It has proved to be one of the most concise, accurate and powerful strategy statements ever made by a corporate executive. For the last decade this strategy has been the engine for GE's growth. Since 1995, it has also provided a consistent answer to the constant question: "Why do Six Sigma, anyway?" At GE, Six Sigma is clearly a competitive tool aimed at strategic business targets.

Notice that Welch's statement was not a "need-to-know" secret. Effective strategic business plans are communicated to all of the company's stakeholders: managers, associates, shareholders, suppliers and customers. Done well, this communication creates a widespread sense of urgency and sets off a chain reaction in which Six Sigma provides a critical "missing link."

SIX SIGMA AS THE "MISSING LINK"

Communicate Strategic Intent
Increases Stakeholder Expectations
Generates Positive Pressure to Improve
Creates the NEED for Systematic Improvement
Six Sigma Fills the NEED
Produces Consistent Improvements

MANAGERS...

Your first priority is to make sure YOU understand the organization's strategic business plan. You know you've "got it" when:

1. You can articulate "The Plan" in terms that everyone working for you can understand.
2. You can communicate how your department/team contributes directly to the key performance goals in the organization-wide plan.

The best way to confirm that both elements are clearly understood is to present them (use a **simple** visual) at any sizeable meeting and ask, *"How can we do better?"*

Intro

Ready?

6 Months

Project

Long Haul

DMAIIC

Tools

R & R

MANAGERS (continued)

As the General Manager of a multi-billion dollar division once said:

> *"I never realized that the most important part of my job would be to repeat our strategy and goals 40 times a day!"*

Besides the "bottom line" plan, people at all levels must believe that Six Sigma is part of the long-term vision and values of the organization. In addition to "walking the talk" every day, a Six Sigma organization must re-enforce its values by:

- Communicating them.
- Actually treating vision and values as "core competencies" and training people in them.
- Auditing them.
- Rewarding those who live up to them, NOT those who disregard them.

If this foundation is in place, then Six Sigma flows *naturally* from these existing values. This "fit" creates instant credibility.

Lesson #2 – *Create the REALITY, not just the "sense," of urgency that depends on Six Sigma's successful implementation.*
Building directly on Lesson #1, leaders must make Six Sigma a BUSINESS priority, rather than "just" a quality improvement initiative. Keep in mind that whenever a new improvement program is introduced, people will ask two basic questions:

1. How important is it relative to everything else within my responsibility?
2. How long is this program going to be around?

Therefore, the leadership team must convince the organization that Six Sigma is both *urgent* AND *ongoing*.

The "Killer Matrix" below illustrates this point.

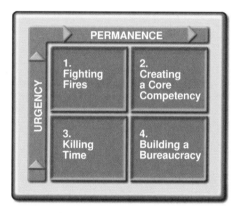

The "Killer" Matrix

Quadrants 1, 3, and 4 "kill" the improvement effort either through frustration or exhaustion. The solution lies in positioning Six Sigma as a core competency developed and sustained in order to be competitive. What are some ways to prove this to a sometimes-skeptical audience?

1. Use real, yet aggressive, numbers when estimating the impact of Six Sigma on key performance measures. Whenever possible, compare your current (and projected) performance with that of your competitors.

2. Involve managers, and other stakeholders, beyond the Executive Team in the planning process. One major U.S. rail carrier not only involved managers, but also union leaders in planning retreats.

3. Emphasize (and re-emphasize) that ALL managers will experience APPLIED training. (See Chapter 3 for a detailed description of the training program for managers under the Green Belt banner.)

4. SHOW THEM THE MONEY! Point to real dollars that have been set aside in the next FY budget.

Intro
Ready?
6 Months
Project
Long Haul
DMAIIC
Tools
R & R

Intro

Ready ?

6 Months

Project

Long Haul

DMAIIC

Tools

R & R

Lesson #3 – Create a Six Sigma implementation plan that's clear and outrageously aggressive (to match the urgency expressed in Lesson #2)

It sounds almost too obvious…create a plan. What's different about this plan is that it combines careful thinking with an uncompromising attitude about achieving seemingly impossible goals. Why spend so much precious executive time and attention on THE PLAN?

- It forces the planners to dig in and understand the connections among the pieces of Six Sigma.

- It creates a realistic picture of the scope and complexity of the effort.

- It specifies the resources needed to do it right AND rapidly.

- It forces the senior management team to look squarely at the commitment that's needed, and either step up to it or walk away. If the team decides to step up to it but individual executives choose to "walk away," those executives should be heading for the nearest door.

- It's a sign of respect for the time commitments and current priorities of the "doers" throughout the organization.

MANAGERS...

You are **not** off the hook even if THE PLAN may have been developed "upstairs" or "at corporate." In order to be a responsible team member you must:

- Give honest feedback, even when the planners don't specifically ask for it.

- Be realistic (based on facts), but open (based on creative solutions).

- Commit to becoming a Six Sigma learner, doer, and teacher.

A Six Sigma implementation plan is the same as any document that introduces a major change. It should include:

- A one-page summary.
- Detail pages supporting each of the major headings in the summary.
- Frequently asked questions (FAQ's).

Think of it as a Web Site with a homepage, linked pages and an FAQ section. In fact, the company Web site is an ideal vehicle to both communicate detailed information and generate a dialogue about concerns, questions and points of confusion.

These points relate to the *form* of communication, but *what* content must be included? It should read like a good newspaper article, covering the *who, what, where, when, why and how much* of the "Six Sigma Story."

Headline	Details
Who will...	...be the <u>Champions</u> for the process? ...serve as <u>Black Belts</u>? ...serve as <u>Green Belts</u>? ...conduct the training? ...be on the teams?
What will Six Sigma...	...work on? ...use as metrics? ...demand of Black Belts? ...demand of Green Belts?
Where will Six Sigma...	...be implemented?
When will Six Sigma...	...be launched? ...be implemented in different divisions/departments?
Why will Six Sigma...	...benefit the entire organization? ...be better or different from past improvement efforts?
How much will Six Sigma...	...cost? ...return on the investment? ...affect the current budget?

The most successful implementations of Six Sigma, such as GE, have taken these implementation plans and added a key ingredient – SPEED.

Jack Welch was willing to ask the organization to make improvements at a seemingly impossible pace. This could have become what Dr. W. Edwards Deming called "arbitrary numerical goals" and "cheerleading." Welch avoided this by providing the implementation plan, plus:

- Training
- Support (Black Belts, infrastructure, etc.)
- Reward
- Personal recognition

Lesson #4 – *Link and build on past improvement efforts, <u>but</u> spell out what will be different AND better.*

Virtually every organization has a history of improvement. The track record of results will ALWAYS be mixed. Projects fail; tools are misapplied; teams disintegrate. It's a natural variation that occurs in any major-change program. Accept this fact and learn from it. It's wise to take the time to do this "post mortem" BEFORE you engage outside consultants and read lots of "how-to" books …except this one, of course.

Things to look for in past efforts…

- Identify your *most* and *least* successful improvement project during the last 12 months and apply the <u>5 Why's</u>. Look for root causes of both success and failure that cut across a number of projects.
- Identify people who have vital technical skills (e.g., in training and project leadership). This builds a pool of available resources and re-enforces the value of past training and experience.
- Look at other major organization-wide change efforts that you've attempted. What's your track record? Why did they work? Why did they fail?
- Find well-documented improvement case studies from WITHIN your organization. Demonstrate that improvement

Intro

Ready?

6 Months

Project

Long Haul

DMAIIC

Tools

R & R

can happen systematically in YOUR organizational culture and NOT just at GE, Allied Signal or other showcase companies.

Things to emphasize about a Six Sigma future...

- Six Sigma is a mix of familiar and new improvement methods.
- Six Sigma is flexible enough to adapt somewhat to the organization's culture, BUT the culture must clearly adapt to Six Sigma. If it doesn't, then the results will simply be a repeat of the past.
- Six Sigma is unabashedly focused on 3 internal targets: lowering costs, increasing productivity, and realizing more profits out of operations.
- Six Sigma will have the biggest financial impact through increased sales to a growing number of loyal customers who will pay for superior value.

MANAGERS...

If senior executives are "Directors of Marketing," then you're the Six Sigma sales force. You must honestly "sell" the change by:

- Staying positive, not being cynical.

- Looking for opportunities to "use the Six Sigma model in your own processes."

- Help members of your team imagine how the operation would change if processes produced only 3.4 defects per million opportunities.

Warning #1 – *Don't act before you've thought it through.*

Traditionally, there are two schools of thought about the ideal pace to introduce quality improvement programs:

1. **Shock the System –** In this approach, the existing system is blown apart and people have to then find a way to stabilize it. It's a high-risk, high-energy experience. *This is the underlying philosophy of <u>Business Process Re-Engineering (BPR)</u>.*

Intro

Ready ?

6 Months

Project

Long Haul

DMAIIC

Tools

R & R

2. Slowly Get Rolling – This approach emphasizes the steady progress by which the change "grows on" the people in the organization. It's assumed that people will get more committed to the change as they get more comfortable with it. Total Quality Management (TQM) generally used this approach.

Based on the lessons learned from both BPR and TQM over the last 15 years, Six Sigma uses an implementation style that could be called "*Shock & Roll.*"

The Shock...	The Roll...
• Create an aggressive implementation schedule. • Set extremely high performance goals. • Require total commitment and active participation by executives and managers.	• Create the plan and stick to it. THE PLAN should dictate which projects are selected, not vice versa. • Carefully choose projects for their strategic impact, but... • Choose first-round projects that will yield quick and sure results. • Choose your "best and brightest" as Black Belts. • Train enough Black Belts to support the scale and pace of the plan. • Don't start training too soon. Apply the skills to real projects ASAP. • Budget to fully support the plan.

Six Sigma is NOT a shoot-from-the-hip process. Aggressive plans must be followed closely and supported enthusiastically by leaders at all levels of the company.

In this preparation phase, everyone is looking for evidence of one thing:

*"IS THIS PLACE **SERIOUS** ABOUT SIX SIGMA?"*

Intro

Ready ?

6 Months

Project

Long Haul

DMAIIC

Tools

R & R

Warning #2 – *Don't make Six Sigma something outside the main-stream of the business.*

The pace of business has increased exponentially over the last 10 years. Decisions, transactions, delivery, feedback from the market have all gone from weeks, to days, to hours and finally, to seconds.

Technology has helped us keep pace with productivity growth at record levels, BUT at the same time companies have become:

- Flatter
- More flexible
- Leaner
- More demanding of results

Unprecedented Pressure to Perform

Six Sigma as a "pressure reliever" – Anything that misses the center of the business target just increases the pressure to perform. The key is to make Six Sigma a "pressure reliever" rather than a "pressure cooker." How?

- Start and end every Six Sigma conversation with the connection between the project(s) and a key company performance measure.
- As discussions about Six Sigma spread, stay focused on problems and processes that are *known* and *nagging* issues.

Black Belts should be specialists, NOT the head coach – It's incredibly important to build a cadre of highly skilled Six Sigma Black Belts. However, they must NOT be placed in charge of the management of the improvement process.  Black Belts are sometimes responsible for managing individual projects, but directing the overall improvement process should be the job of management. Don't just keep managers *engaged in* the process, keep them *in charge of* the process by:

- Dedicating the majority of the budget to training and supporting managers in their role as Green Belts.

Intro

Ready ?

6 Months

Project

Long Haul

DMAIIC

Tools

R & R

- Not creating a large Six Sigma department.
- Involving managers in the "construction plan" for Six Sigma implementation. Think of it as a rolling re-construc tion project on the structure of the company. It's like an "urban renewal" project in which each building on the block is tackled, starting with the one that's in the worst condition.

Spillover Advice

In this section, the key *Lesson sand Warnings* from Six Sigma experts were included in the book. Other important *Lessons and Warnings* are listed below. Once in the e-book, just click on the idea icon next to the *Lessons or Warnings* # you want to view in its entirety.

Lesson #5 – *Do whatever it takes to create a deep understanding of, and commitment to, Six Sigma within the top leadership team.*

Lesson #6 – *Link Six Sigma to current corporate initiatives (e.g. Baldrige, ISO, Leadership models).*

Warning #3 – *Don't allow management actions that are contrary to the stated Six Sigma values.*

Warning #4 – *Don't publicly over-sell Six Sigma.*

✓ Check List:

Have you…

- ❑ Convincingly made the Business Case for Six Sigma that works at all levels in the organization?

- ❑ Built a consensus within the leadership team that Six Sigma is a key to your competitive future?

- ❑ Created a credible implementation plan that addresses both your business targets and Six Sigma as a vehicle for achieving them?

- ❑ Put "your money where your mouth is" in a budget that holds up under close scrutiny?

- ❑ Involved line managers in a meaningful way?

- ❑ Created excitement about a Six Sigma future?

Intro

Ready ?

6 Months

Project

Long Haul

DMAIIC

Tools

R & R

Chapter 3:
The First 6 Months

A Six Sigma implementation process that quickly creates powerful results AND lasting commitment.

Purpose of this chapter:

To lay out a step-by-step plan for launching a typical Six Sigma program. It focuses on the crucial first 6 months of implementation during which the tone of the Six Sigma process is set. It must be seen by all of the stakeholders as both *exciting* (dramatic business impact) and *long lasting* (a way-of-life).

For senior executives this chapter...

- Describes in detail the workload that the implementation of Six Sigma will place on the organization.
- Provides a clear process for selecting first round Six Sigma projects that are both *powerful* (significant results) and *practical* (attainable).
- Highlight the type and scale of results that you can expect during the first months of implementation.
- Detail the tasks that only you can do to ensure that the implementation will be a complete success.

For managers at all levels this chapter...

- Describes how you and the rest of the organization will be trained to lead and participate in Six Sigma project teams.
- Removes the mystery of what it means to "do Six Sigma" on a daily basis.

 **Big Picture:**

The Launch

Now that the commitment to Six Sigma has been made, a key decision for the Executive Team is:

> *Do we launch Six Sigma with a big splash or with a business-like announcement?*

Intro

Ready ?

6 Months

Project

Long Haul

DMAIIC

Tools

R & R

A lesson from the 80's...

Picture a fire engine carrying senior executives AND a Dixieland band driving past the assembly line of a major U. S. automotive company. The banner on the side of the truck screamed "ZERO DEFECTS." Finally, picture the assemblers (in unison) turning their back on the passing parade. What's wrong with this picture?

The first 6 months should be about building a solid foundation, while moving quickly and decisively and NOT about hoopla and hype. The most successful companies have treated Six Sigma like other *company-wide strategic objectives* for which people and business units are held accountable for their performance (or lack thereof.) However, one message must be conveyed (in whatever style works in your culture):

> **Six Sigma WILL happen and participation is NOT an optional activity.**

The Goals

❑ To train a cadre of Black Belts and Green Belts through hands-on application of the Six Sigma process and tools AND to recover the money spent on training.

❑ To establish the credibility of Six Sigma as a process that moves your business' Key Performance Indicators (KPI's).

❑ To demonstrate leadership in making systematic process improvement a permanent part of your organization's culture.

❑ To create documented examples that prove that Six Sigma works in YOUR business.

❑ To create a tracking and communications system that allows the ENTIRE organization to see the status and results of any Six Sigma project at anytime.

Intro

Ready ?

6 Months

Project

Long Haul

DMAIIC

Tools

R & R

> *The PRIMARY goal of the first six months is to ensure that Six Sigma has the greatest possible impact on the bottom-line of the business in the shortest possible time.*

The Bottom Line

What type of financial return can you expect following the first six months of implementation? Let's make some assumptions based upon a company with 5000 employees:

- The target is ten Black Belts per 1000 employees and one Master Black belt for every 15-20 Black Belts.
- The average Black Belt assignment is 2 years.
- The target is to have the full complement of 50 Black Belts within 2 years. Therefore, you must train and certify 8-10 Black Belts every 6 months.
- It costs an average of $30,000 and $45,000 to train a Black Belt and Master Black Belt, respectively. Green Belt training costs an average of $7,500 per person.
- The average savings per Black Belt project is $150,000 (the lowest estimate we've seen).

The Numbers...		
$1.5 Million in Revenue Savings	**$520K in Training Costs**	**$980K** ** **Profit Increase**
• 10 projects @ $150K ave.*	• $300K (10 Black Belts @ $30K) • $45K (1 Master Black Belt) • $75K (10 Green Belts @ $7,500) • $100K (Exec. Team, Champion, Associates/ Proj. Teams)	
* See top of following page		** See top of following page

Intro

Ready ?

6 Months

Project

Long Haul

DMAIIC

Tools

R & R

* This does not reflect any Green Belt projects or more indirect savings/revenue resulting from educated employees and/or cultural changes.

** This assumes that there were no capital investments made as part of the projects.

The Structure

During the first six months an organizational structure must be built that supports the work of the first-round projects. But it must also be strong enough to support the exponential growth in Six Sigma projects that will follow. How do you prevent a "necessary and sufficient" structure from becoming an "improvement bureaucracy"?

At an internal management forum, Jack Welch was asked about the danger of a Six Sigma bureaucracy. His reply…

> *"I don't give a damn if we get a little bureaucracy as long as we get the results. If it bothers you, yell at it. Kick it. Scream at it. Break it!"*
>
> <u>Business Week</u>, *June 8, 1998*

Following is a "typical" Six Sigma organizational chart. Your organization may not have all of the roles listed, but someone, by whatever title you choose, must be responsible for the *functions and tasks* listed under each role. In smaller organizations, it's likely that one person would take on multiple roles. However, if you focus on these necessary tasks you'll build a Six Sigma "support system," NOT a Six Sigma bureaucracy.

Intro

Ready ?

6 Months

Project

Long Haul

DMAIIC

Tools

R & R

Roles and Responsibilities in a Six Sigma Program

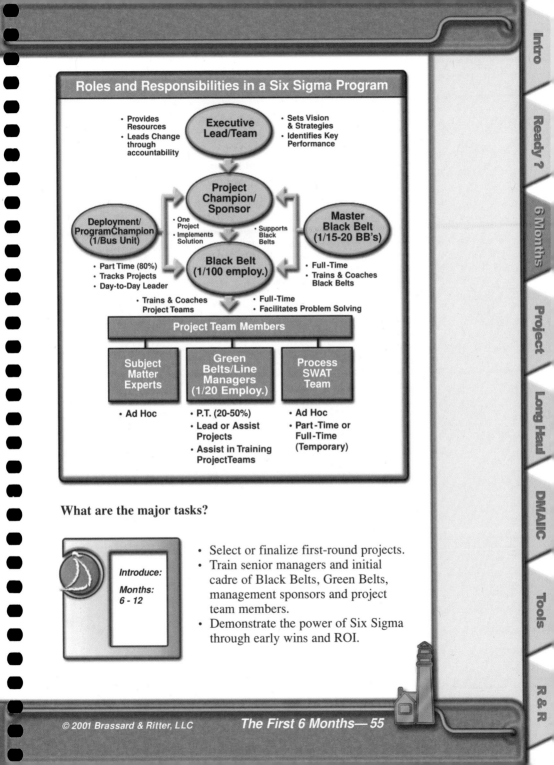

- Provides Resources
- Leads Change through accountability

Executive Lead/Team

- Sets Vision & Strategies
- Identifies Key Performance

Project Champion/ Sponsor

Deployment/ ProgramChampion (1/Bus Unit)

- One Project
- Implements Solution

- Supports Black Belts

Master Black Belt (1/15-20 BB's)

- Part Time (80%)
- Tracks Projects
- Day-to-Day Leader

Black Belt (1/100 employ.)

- Full-Time
- Trains & Coaches Black Belts

- Trains & Coaches Project Teams
- Full-Time
- Facilitates Problem Solving

Project Team Members

Subject Matter Experts	Green Belts/Line Managers (1/20 Employ.)	Process SWAT Team
• Ad Hoc	• P.T. (20-50%) • Lead or Assist Projects • Assist in Training ProjectTeams	• Ad Hoc • Part-Time or Full-Time (Temporary)

What are the major tasks?

Introduce:

Months: 6 - 12

- Select or finalize first-round projects.
- Train senior managers and initial cadre of Black Belts, Green Belts, management sponsors and project team members.
- Demonstrate the power of Six Sigma through early wins and ROI.

Training is the heart of the first 6 months, but don't mistake it for any theory-laden, classroom experience you've ever had. Six Sigma is about applied learning.

- The Executive Team and Champions immediately select projects and Black Belt and Green Belt candidates.

- Black Belts and Green Belts alternate training with project team work for the entire life of their projects.

- Project team members "learn as they go" through just-in-time training provided by the Black Belts.

All of the other components of the program (Reviews, communications, etc.) that surround the project teams are designed to MAKE THE TRAINING AND THE PROJECT TEAMS PRODUCE MAXIMUM RESULTS. The following Responsibility Flow Chart puts all of the pieces together:

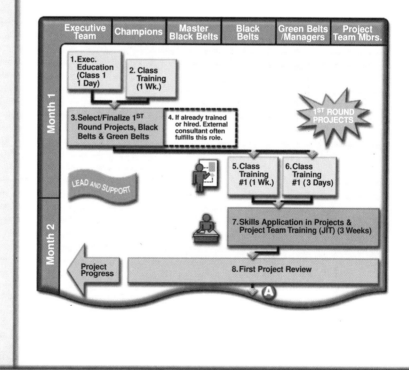

Intro

Ready ?

6 Months

Project

Long Haul

DMAIIC

Tools

R & R

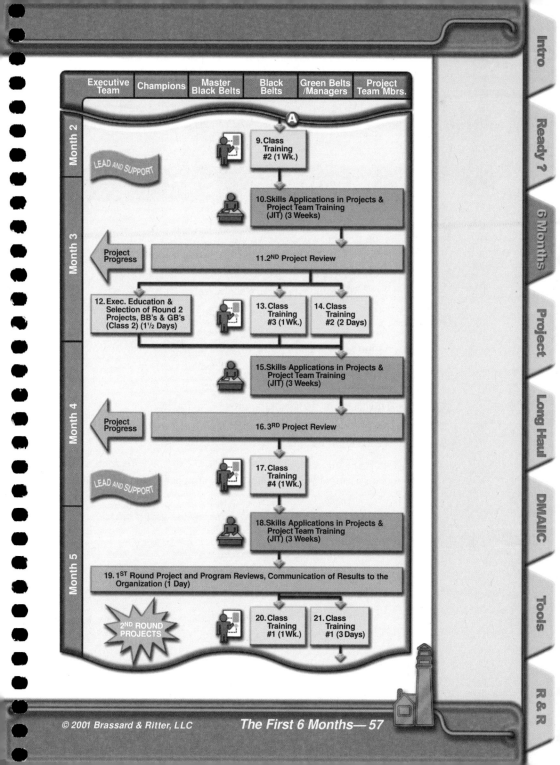

Intro

Ready ?

6 Months

Project

Long Haul

DMAIIC

Tools

R & R

Executive Team	Champions	Master Black Belts	Black Belts	Green Belts /Managers	Project Team Mbrs.

A

Month 2

LEAD AND SUPPORT

9. Class Training #2 (1 Wk.)

10. Skills Applications in Projects & Project Team Training (JIT) (3 Weeks)

Month 3

Project Progress

11. 2ND Project Review

12. Exec. Education & Selection of Round 2 Projects, BB's & GB's (Class 2) (1½ Days)

13. Class Training #3 (1 Wk.)

14. Class Training #2 (2 Days)

15. Skills Applications in Projects & Project Team Training (JIT) (3 Weeks)

Month 4

Project Progress

16. 3RD Project Review

LEAD AND SUPPORT

17. Class Training #4 (1 Wk.)

18. Skills Applications in Projects & Project Team Training (JIT) (3 Weeks)

Month 5

19. 1ST Round Project and Program Reviews, Communication of Results to the Organization (1 Day)

2ND ROUND PROJECTS

20. Class Training #1 (1 Wk.)

21. Class Training #1 (3 Days)

Intro

Ready ?

6 Months

Project

Long Haul

DMAIIC

Tools

R & R

The following section provides detail of what occurs at each implementation step. The numbers refer to the corresponding step in the Responsibility Flow Chart above. The activities that recur during the process or that involve the same role (e.g. Black Belts, Green Belts, etc.) are grouped together.

1. Executive Education – Session #1 (1 Day)

This is the first of two executive education sessions. The second is held at the end of the third month of first round implementation. The first session helps the Executive team to understand:

- The evolution of the theory and methods of Six Sigma.
- The meaning of "Six Sigma Thinking."
- The financial and operational reasons for practicing Six Sigma in ALL parts of the organization.
- The impact of a Six Sigma capability vs. a Three Sigma capability in a process they manage.
- The basics of the DMAIIC process and tools.
- The Six Sigma implementation model and their role and responsibilities within it.

Most immediately, the session prepares the Executive Team to make the 4 decisions that will have the greatest impact on the short- and long-term success of Six Sigma:

These decisions signal how ambitious the program targets will be & how serious leaders are about hitting those targets.

1. *What projects will be tackled during the first 6 months of implementation?*
2. *Who will be the Six Sigma Champions?*
3. *Who will be the first-round Black Belt candidates?*
4. *Are we REALLY committed to making Six Sigma work?*

2. Champion Classroom Training (1 Week)

Champions are the key program planners. They are the ones really responsible for developing and implementing the detailed "Roll-Out Plan" that includes:

- Identifying the biggest opportunities.
- Establishing goals and expectations.
- Creating tangible and intangible incentives for teams and their leaders.

Deployment or Program Champion – Normally a senior vice-president, director or vice-president who:

- Is the CEO's designee to manage the Six Sigma program on a day-to-day basis.
- Runs interference for the program as it becomes part of the management system.
- Makes sure that money, people and equipment are flowing smoothly to support implementation.

Project Champions/Sponsors – Typically are business-unit/division level executives who:

- Prioritize "local" issues that the program needs to tackle.
- Create detailed program implementation plans for their unit or facility.
- Work on any cross-functional issues that the program surfaces.
- Work directly with Black Belts (and Master Black Belts when they're in place) to make sure that they have what they need to succeed.
- Are ultimately accountable for the results of the project team(s) that they sponsor.

Training Outline

Both types of Champions need to understand the basic Six Sigma Process and tools as well as the managerial challenge of introducing a significant culture change. Following are the main topics covered in the 5-day Champions course:

Intro
Ready ?
6 Months
Project
Long Haul
DMAIIC
Tools
R & R

Champion Training – Month 1

Champion Classroom Training (1 week)

Leading the Planning and Implementation of Six Sigma

General & Overview Topics:

Champion Skill Areas

A System for Managing (1 module)
Assessing your organization's current performance measures and how the Six Sigma system and principles will dramatically improve those measures.

Business Planning (1 module)
Building a Balanced Scorecard and a Deployment Tree Diagram that shows the connection of strategic objectives to Six Sigma projects.

Leading Six Sigma (1 module)
Using cost-of-poor-quality analysis to select high-return projects and creating progress indicators that Champions use when reviewing Six Sigma projects.

Process Scorekeeping (2 modules)
The basics of Process Management, including the identification of process indicators (outcome and upstream), setting performance targets and ongoing process control plans.

Interpreting Data (1 module)
Practical introduction to process variation and the core statistical tools that project teams use to create "Six Sigma processes."

Bringing Existing Processes to Six Sigma Performance: DMAIIC (3 modules)
Step-by-step training in applying the DMAIIC problem solving model, using the DMAIIC Storyboard as the guide.

Creating New Products/Processes for Six Sigma Performance: DMEDVI (1 module)
Introduction to the DMEDVI development model that's used by project teams when creating a new product or process with Six Sigma performance designed into it.

Intro

Ready ?

6 Months

Project

Long Haul

DMAIIC

Tools

R & R

3. Select or finalize the first-round projects, Black Belts and Green Belts

A. **The Projects**

In the Diagnosis and Planning phase described in Chapter 2, the Executive Team made 2 decisions that prepare the way for first-round projects selection:

1. The selection of the "focus areas" for improvement that will have the biggest impact on the company's growth strategy. These are NOT generally specific projects.

2. The scale and timing of the Six Sigma roll-out. For example, the initial implementation plan will fund 10 first-round Black Belt projects (obviously this number will vary considerably, based on the size of the company and the program budget).

Prior to the Executive Team and the Champions' initial education/working session, a smaller working group or members of the Quality staff break the focus areas (such as "Reduce Warrantee Costs") into project-size opportunities. They also meet with managers to review their performance data and potential Six Sigma projects.

The Criteria

Both those who are working "off-line" to identify first-round projects and the Executive Team must apply clear and consistent criteria when making the final selections.

Any Six Sigma project must pass through *Filter #1:*

> **A strong connection and contribution to the business growth strategy.**

However, because the first round projects are so critical for the long-term success of the program, first-round projects must also meet **two additional sets of minimum requirements**:

> *Start in the hottest growth areas with strong leaders. Go for great results AND PR!*

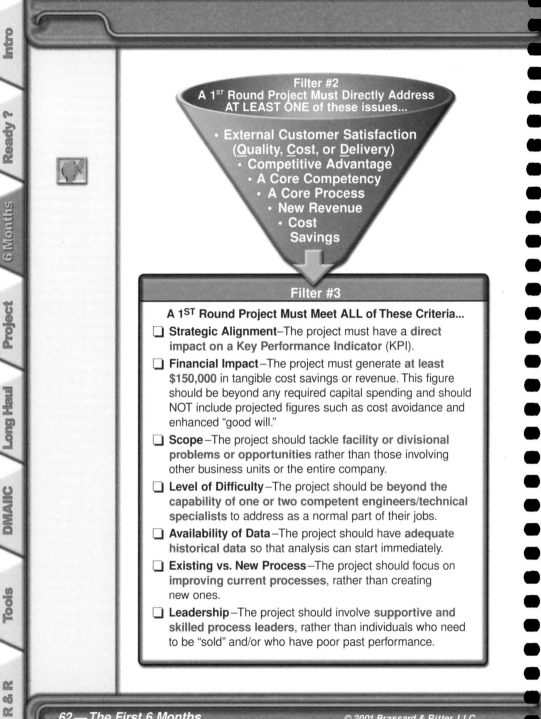

Filter #2
A 1ST Round Project Must Directly Address
AT LEAST ONE of these issues...

- **External Customer Satisfaction**
(<u>Q</u>uality, <u>C</u>ost, or <u>D</u>elivery)
- **Competitive Advantage**
- **A Core Competency**
- **A Core Process**
- **New Revenue**
- **Cost
Savings**

Filter #3

A 1ST Round Project Must Meet ALL of These Criteria...

☐ **Strategic Alignment**–The project must have a **direct impact on a Key Performance Indicator** (KPI).

☐ **Financial Impact**–The project must generate **at least $150,000** in tangible cost savings or revenue. This figure should be beyond any required capital spending and should NOT include projected figures such as cost avoidance and enhanced "good will."

☐ **Scope**–The project should tackle **facility or divisional problems or opportunities** rather than those involving other business units or the entire company.

☐ **Level of Difficulty**–The project should be **beyond the capability of one or two competent engineers/technical specialists** to address as a normal part of their jobs.

☐ **Availability of Data**–The project should have **adequate historical data** so that analysis can start immediately.

☐ **Existing vs. New Process**–The project should focus on **improving current processes**, rather than creating new ones.

☐ **Leadership**–The project should involve **supportive and skilled process leaders**, rather than individuals who need to be "sold" and/or who have poor past performance.

Intro
Ready ?
6 Months
Project
Long Haul
DMAIIC
Tools
R & R

Based on these criteria, consider the following two examples:

A plant of a major automotive supplier saved $250,000 by reducing its internal scrap rate. Defect rates at key production steps dropped by as much as 50%.

A successful Six Sigma project AND a good first round product choice…

- A single facility focus.
- Generated a significant and noticeable cost savings.
- Had a major impact on customer satisfaction.
- Scrap data was readily available
- Used a range of improvement tools.

An international heavy-equipment manufacturer chose a braising process problem that was causing production delays.

A solid Six Sigma project, but not an ideal first round choice…

- A multi-plant, multi-process problem.
- Available data was not useful; useful data was not available.
- Took over a year to show results due to the need for multiple experiments.
- A long-standing issue that had defied solution in the past.

Both projects were noteworthy accomplishments, but the automotive scrap rate reduction project struck just the right balance of *business significance, attainability* and *predictability*. There is no list of "perfect projects" but here are some typical ones that also meet these criteria.

Project	Impact
• Increase dryer throughput (Mgf.)*	$130K
• Reduce freight costs (Shipping)*	$700K
• Warranty reduction (Mfg.)	$150K
• Reduce cost of waste disposal (Environ.)*	$320K
• Reduce time to issue bills by 50% (Acct.)	$2.6Mill.
• Direct Mat. Variation Cost Reduction. (Mfg.)	$172K
• Implement Forecasting Model (Sales)	$500K
• Reduce obsolete inventory (Product. Plng.)	$1.7Mill.
• Increase warehouse output by 100%	$250K
(9 to 18 items/hr)* Reduced travel costs*	$1.3Mill.

* From *Six Sigma and Its Impact on American Business,* a presentation by Ronald D. Snee, Sigma Breakthrough Technologies, Inc. October 17, 2000

B. Selecting or finalizing the First-Round Black Belts and Green Belts

The Black Belts

The Executive Team and Champions have the tough job of selecting Black Belts who must be both technical experts and skilled project leaders. What are these almost-mystical Black Belts? What roles do they play? What skills do they need?

The Black Belt Job Description:

A full-time individual, skilled in quality improvement systems and tools, who trains, leads and supports Six Sigma problem-solving teams in measuring, analyzing, improving and controlling processes critical to both customer satisfaction and profitability.

- Usually a two year assignment.

- Assigned to their "home" business unit.

- Has the authority to drive the project to completion, rather than acting as a facilitator with limited authority.

- Required to play a number of leadership roles in supporting projects and project team members.

Intro

Ready ?

6 Months

Project

Long Haul

DMAIC

Tools

R & R

The Black Belt Role Grid

Responsible for Creating Capabilities	Responsible for Project Tasks		
	Coach	Mentor	
	Teacher		Project Leader
	Best Practitioner		Content Expert

A Black Belt must be equally comfortable in each of these roles in order to be effective. A Black Belt's days are typically filled with:

- Ongoing work sessions to help project leaders (and team members) develop their individual skills and their project work. *(Mentor)*

- Impromptu one-on-one meetings with rookie project leaders. *(Coach)*

- Formal and informal training sessions. *(Teacher)*

- Project team meetings. *(Project Leader)*

- Broadcasting an e-mail on a new tool application. *(Best Practitioner)*

- Hands-on analytical work. *(Content Expert)*

Typical Black Belt Distribution of Time (in a "mature" Six Sigma program)

% of Black Belt Time

Project Leader	Coach	Expert	Mentor	Teacher	Best Practitioner
25	20	20	15	10	10

Intro

Ready ?

6 Months

Project

Long Haul

DMAIC

Tools

R & R

The Black Belt Skill Set

An effective Black Belt brings a mix of personality, natural abilities and skills gained through training.

Analytical Skills...*to bring meaning to data.*

- Customer Research
- Measuring Performance and Variability
- Process Management & Analysis
- Stratification and Prioritization
- Formal Hypothesis Testing
- Measuring Relationships among Variables
- Design Management
- Reliability Management
- Production Management

Leadership Qualities & Skills...*to bring people up to the challenge.*

- Self-starter
- Passionate
- Learner
- Good communicator (oral/written/electronic)
- Thick-skinned
- Able to maintain organizational focus on the project despite competing priorities
- Team Facilitator (not dictator)
- Highly respected by the organization for past performance
- Detailed knowledge of the business
- Politically savvy
- Ambitious
- Trusted leader

Project Management Skills... *to bring discipline to the project.*

- Chartering projects
- Identifying deliverables and project risks
- Planning and conducting reviews
- Planning the project schedule, including the Critical Path

A Tale of Two Black belts: *Different Backgrounds, Same Passion*

This is an interview with two people with a common passion… their new roles as Black Belts at New Hampshire Ball Bearing, a 1200-person wholly owned subsidiary of NMB, USA. Dianne Moulton and Alan Pelletier are part of the third wave of Black Belts trained at NHBB over the last year and a half. Dianne is the full-time coordinator of all of the Black Belts and Alan splits his time between Black Belt work (2 days/week) and his machining position.

What's been most helpful in your background?

Dianne: I've worked in office administration and most recently as an Associate Engineer, but probably my work as a police dispatcher has helped me the most as a Black Belt. A dispatcher has to size up a situation quickly by focusing on the important facts. This has proved to be really helpful as a Black Belt when I'm faced with mountains of data.

Alan: Believe me, as a machine set-up and operator, and now a toolmaker, I feel that I have an in-depth understanding of the machining process. This reinforces my ability to understand problems and my credibility in dealing with them.

What are the important things that a Black Belt brings?

Alan: A work ethic…the willingness to work hard and show commitment to the project… that you'll do whatever it takes to help the team succeed. At the same time, you have to reinforce that since this is a team effort that everyone has to support each other in getting things done.

Dianne: Because I come primarily from a non-technical background I can ask the "dumb questions" and get people thinking about the basics. A Black Belt also has to be incredibly positive with a "We can do this!" attitude. I've found that a positive attitude can be contagious.

Intro

Ready ?

6 Months

Project

Long Haul

DMAIIC

Tools

R & R

Intro

Ready ?

6 Months

Project

Long Haul

DMAIIC

Tools

R & R

Signs of a winning project?

Dianne: What I look for is whether it's a well-qualified problem. First, is there some history that will provide good data? Secondly, is the difference between the current status and the goal significant? Is the process ongoing to allow testing and analysis? If the answer is "no" to any of these, let's find something else to tackle.

Alan: I look for data and commitment…a solid, well-documented history of the problem and solid commitment from the stakeholders. They have to show their commitment by spending their time in the meetings, providing information and asking about progress. Could I add that I also look for a team that's open to change, learning and adapting to a Six Sigma approach. A project is tough enough without having to pull a team along that's kicking and screaming the whole time.

What's your favorite project?

Alan: My first project was the best so far because it was such an amazing combination of learning and seeing results at the same time. On the first project alone, we did seven DOE's! I saw that there were actually only a few inputs that really had a significant impact on the process. That flew in the face of 25 years of machining experience. It was an eye-opener!

Dianne: I honestly don't have one because every project is so interesting. As a Black Belt I get to shape and redefine the project based on what the data shows. That unpredictability makes my job challenging and satisfying.

What's next for you?

Dianne: I'd like to continue this role for my whole career because of the satisfaction that I just talked about. The project work itself can be pretty intense, so I do appreciate the variety that my coordinator's role gives me. It's a great balance that I think I'll enjoy for a long, long time.

Alan: I like the fact that I'm still working as an operator 3 days a week. It gives me the same kind of balance that Dianne was talking about. It also keeps me in touch with the operation and how it really runs day-to-day. I think that combination makes me even more effective as a Black Belt. But I wouldn't mind a temporary full-time assignment to a particularly intense project for, say, 3 months or so. That could be fun.

Intro

Ready ?

6 Months

Project

Long Haul

DMAIIC

Tools

R & R

> ⚓ **Executive Team...**
>
> The most successful Black Belts have often been strongest in the leadership category, even at the expense of statistical knowledge. You can transfer the statistical skills, but leadership skills are another matter. Lists of Black Belt skills and qualities also describe a manager/ leader on the rise in your organization. Do you believe enough in the power of Six Sigma to make this "rising star" a full-time Black Belt? HINT: Never answer a rhetorical question!

The Green Belts

The selection process for Green Belts is more straightforward than that for Black Belts. Since the ideal model is to provide training at the time that it's needed, only those managers who will play a role in the first-round projects should be initially trained as Green Belts.* They will tend to be strong candidates anyway since one of the criteria for selecting first-round projects is that the managers involved are "supportive and skilled."

A Green Belt ...

- Works on Six Sigma projects on a part-time basis.

- Leads project teams that are *smaller scale* (e.g. single process/department) and that use *simpler problem-solving tools*.

- Assists Black Belts in problem solving and project team training.

- Calls in the Black Belts to act as a coach or expert in complex projects and advanced methods.

- Works with the Black Belt in assembling the project documentation, such as the <u>DMAIIC Story</u>.

* Some companies do business unit-wide G.B. training during the first round. To make this work, provide resources to support ALL of their projects

> ## Managers...
>
>
> *In the short term, use your role as a Green Belt to show dedication to the process and to model behavior. Show your belief in the principles of Six Sigma thinking by making operational decisions that reinforce these beliefs.*
>
> *After the first round, you will also drive the pace and impact of Six Sigma in your area by:*
>
> - *Identifying the KPI's for the process(es) that you own*
>
> - *Selecting the highest leverage issues and projects to tackle in your area*
>
> - *Freeing up (and supporting) your best people to work on the project teams*

4. The Role and Relationships of the Master Black Belt

A Dose of Common Sensei

A "sensei" in the world of martial arts is a highly respected teacher or mentor. A sensei not only has skill, but wisdom. He or she uses that wisdom to guide others who are dedicated to improving themselves and their skills. A Master Black Belt is a Six Sigma Sensei.

The Master Black Belt is one of the most critical roles for the *long-term success* of a Six Sigma program. A typical Master Black Belt:

- Trains, coaches, mentors and certifies Black Belts.

- Develops new training materials.

- Helps to select new projects.

- Supports the Champions and Executive Team in accelerating Six Sigma implementation.

- Reviews and tracks progress across all projects.

- Tests and integrates new improvement tools.
- Helps spread best practices.
- Leads large, multifunctional projects.

Having someone of this caliber from the first day of implementation presents tremendous advantages, but individuals with the needed skills are pretty rare.

So what happens when a company doesn't have such a resource available internally or can't recruit someone externally? For the first six to twelve months the external consultant can fill this role. Over this time Consultants work with the Executive Team and Champions to identify Master Black Belt candidates from among the first-round Black Belts.

> At least one Master Black Belt candidate must be *identified* by the end of the first six months and certified by the end of the first year, AT THE LATEST.

To be certified, a Master Black Belt must complete 2 weeks of training beyond the basic Black Belt course along with at least two Black Belt projects. The additional training focuses on long-term program planning, advanced statistical improvement tools, training skills, and techniques for managing complex projects.

If Master Black Belts are identified in the pre-launch phase (in Chapter 2), candidates could already be trained in both the basic Black Belt course as well as in the additional training described below. If the organization is "growing" Master Black Belts from the initial group of Black Belts, this "extra" training often occurs after the first round of projects is completed.

Master Black Belt Training

Master Black Belt Training – 2 weeks in addition to Basic Black Belt 4-week course	**Role/Responsibilities** • In-depth understanding of the certification requirements for all of the Six Sigma leadership roles

Master Black Belt Training – 2 weeks in addition to Basic Black Belt 4-week course

Taking on the Six Sigma Leadership Challenge

General & Overview Topics:

- Integrating Strategic Business Planning and Six Sigma
- Sustaining a Six Sigma Culture
- Change Management

Role/Responsibilities
- In-depth understanding of the certification requirements for all of the Six Sigma leadership roles

Training Skills
- Basics of the train-the-trainer educational approach to teaching Six Sigma
- Incoming skills assessment
- Adult learning practices
- Delivery skills
- Learning assessment

Advanced Statistical Improvement Tools
- More complex experimental techniques
- Enhanced process modeling

Strategic Business Planning
- Developing new performance indicators
- Creating and maintaining performance tracking systems
- Advanced cost analysis techniques
- Scenario building

Project Management
- PERT analysis
- Critical Path Method (CPM)
- Contingency planning
- Creating and coordinating milestones
- Productive Reviews

Change Management
- Psychology of change
- Negotiation skills
- Harnessing teams for change

5, 9, 13, & 17. Black Belt Training Classes #1-4 (Each Class is 1 week)

Training Outline

The Black Belt candidates begin a 4-month cycle of formal classroom training combined with project work. The training sessions and 3-week project work cycles are organized around the DMAIIC steps:

Session 1: *Define & Measure*
- A well-designed team with a well-defined project plan.
- A project problem statement based upon a deep understanding of the current process and its capabilities.

Session 2: *Analyze & Improve*
- Root Cause(s) of the problem that have been validated by facts.
- A cost-effective action plan to eliminate or dramatically reduce the impact of the root cause.

Session 3: *Implement & Control*
- A planned change process that works.
- A Process for Maintaining Improvements.

Session 4: *Design for Six Sigma*
- New products or processes designed with 6σ capability built-in.

Following are the topics and tools covered in the four 5-day Black Belt courses:

Intro
Ready?
6 Months
Project
Long Haul
DMAIIC
Tools
R & R

Black Belt Training – MONTH 1

5. Black Belt Training–Class #1 (1 week)
Introduction to Problem Solving & Identifying the Problem: DEFINE and MEASURE

Helpful Software Skills/ Prerequisites: Microsoft *Office*, Microsoft *Project* (or comparable Project Management software) Microsoft *Visio* (or comparable drawing/charting software)

Role/Responsibilities
- Qualification/Certification Plan

Customer
- Voice of Customer Feedback

Measurement/Data Collection
- Developing Indicators
- Basic Data Collection
- Measurement System Analysis
- Calculating current process (rolled throughput) yield

Project Management
- Project Chartering

Statistical/Problem Solving
- Run Charts
- Sampling
- Histograms
- Process Capability (including Six Sigma)
- Process Flow Charts
- Process Analysis Methods
- Bar Charts
- Pie Charts
- Radar Charts
- Cause and Effect Analysis
- Pareto Analysis

Black Belt Training – MONTH 2

9. Black Belt Training–Class #2 (1 week)
Identifying Root Causes and Solutions: ANALYZE and IMPROVE

Helpful Software Skills/ Prerequisites: Minitab Statistical Software (or comparable SPC software)

Relationships between Variables
- Contingency Analysis
- Scatter Diagrams
- Correlation Analysis
- Regression Analysis – Simple, Linear

Finding the Significance of Process Differences or Changes
- Probability Distributions
- Hypothesis Testing
- Parameter Estimation & Confidence Intervals
- Sampling

Reliability
- Reliability Terms and Definitions
- Reliability Management
- Failure Modes & Effects Analysis
- Fault Tree Analysis
- Weibull Analysis

Experimentation
- Single Factor Experiments

Statistical/Problem Solving
- Cause & Effect Analysis

Black Belt Training – MONTH 3

13. Black Belt Training–Class #3 (1 week) *Making Improvements a Permanent Part of the System: IMPLEMENT and CONTROL*	**Selecting and Implementing Process Changes** • Cost-Benefit Analysis • Evaluating the Effects of Changes/ Standardization & Replication **Managing Improved Processes** • Controlling Processes • Process Management Charts **Statistical/Problem Solving** • Control Charts • Process Capability (including Six Sigma) • Measurement System Analysis
Helpful Software Skills/ Prerequisites:	

Black Belt Training – MONTH 4

17. Black Belt Training–Class #4 (1 week) *Designing and Delivering New Products, Services & Processes: DFSS and Planning Tools*	**Mastering the DMEDVI Model** (<u>D</u>efine, <u>M</u>easure, <u>E</u>xplore, <u>D</u>esign, <u>V</u>alidate, <u>I</u>mplement) **Understanding the Customer** • Obtaining Voice of the Customer • Developing Product/Service Requirements – QFD **Advanced Experimentation Methods** • Analysis of Variation (ANOVA) • Design of Experiments • Taguchi Approach to Design **Reliability Management** • Reliability Testing • Accelerated Testing **Generating New Product/Service Concepts** • Creativity Methods • Performance & Process Benchmarking • Pugh Concept Design Selection • Tolerance Development & Analysis
Helpful Software Skills/ Prerequisites:	

Intro

Ready ?

6 Months

Project

Long Haul

DMAIIC

Tools

R & R

6 & 14. Green Belt Training Classes #1 and 2 (3 Days and 2 Days respectively)

Training Outline

The outline below may appear actually more detailed than that of the Black Belt. However, Green Belts receive approximately 40 hours of training, while Black Belts are generally provided 160 hours of training. By necessity, all of the topics and tools are covered in much less detail.

Green Belt Training – MONTH 1

6. Green Belt Training–Class #1 (3 Days) *Introduction to Six Sigma, the Green Belt Role and the DMAIIC Model and Toolkit*	**DEFINE** • Selection of Projects • Project Chartering • Evaluation Grids • SWOT Analysis • GANTT Chart • Calculating current process (rolled throughput) yield
General & Overview Topics: • Overview of Six Sigma Purpose and Processes • Training plan for all of the Six Sigma roles • Responsibilities of all Six Sigma roles during the life of a project • Baldrige Criteria • How to identify significant performance gaps • How to use performance gaps to generate potential Six Sigma projects	**MEASURE** • Voice of the Customer • Measuring Performance & Variability • Process Management and Analysis • Stratification and Prioritization • Core Customer Research methods • Process Performance Indicators • Data Collection and Display • Six Sigma Scales & Calculating Six Sigma • Flow Chart, Value Add Analysis • Pareto, Histogram, Bar & Pie Charts **ANALYZE** • Foundations of Probability and Statistics • Understanding Variation • Control Charts (introduction to purpose, uses and interpretation) • Cause and Effect Analysis and Verification • Scatter Diagrams *...continued on next page*

Intro
Ready ?
6 Months
Project
Long Haul
DMAIIC
Tools
R & R

Green Belt Training – MONTH 1

continued...

IMPROVE
- Generating and Selecting Countermeasures
- Basics of Cost/Benefit Analysis
- Action Planning
- Defining Deliverables

IMPLEMENT
- Change Management Techniques
- Team Facilitation and Management

CONTROL
- Process Control Systems
- Operating Reviews
- Project Scorecard
- Process Control Plan

Green Belt Training – MONTH 3

14. Green Belt Training–Class #2 (2 Days)
Supporting Six Sigma and Designing and Delivering New Products, Services, & Processes

General & Overview Topics:
- Sustaining a Six Sigma culture
- Six Sigma team issues

Managing Through Six Sigma
- Leading Project Reviews
- Socratic Approach to Project Reviews
- Process Questions for Project Reviews
- Scheduling, Organizing and Conducting Project Reviews
- Project Tracking Methods
- Key leadership skills to maintain a Six Sigma environment

DFSS
- Introduction to techniques for new product and process design
  - Gathering and understanding customer needs
  - Overview of QFD
  - Basic principles of Designed Experiments
  - Creativity methods for generating new product and process concepts
- Supporting DMEDVI (Define, Measure, Explore, Design, Validate, Implement)

Intro

Ready ?

6 Months

Project

Long Haul

DMAIIC

Tools

R & R

7, 10, 15, & 18. Skills Application in Projects and Project Team Training (JIT) – 3 Weeks

During the 3 weeks following each training session, Black Belts are doing hands-on project analysis, leading the team or helping Green

Belts and team members to complete the tasks in each DMAIIC step. The project team members get just enough of the "how-to" to take on assignments and fully participate in problem-solving discussion. Following are typical concepts and tools that project team members learn and apply.

Project Team Member Training – MONTH 1-4

7, 10, 15, 18. Project Team Member Training (Delivered "just-in-time") General & Overview Topics: • Overview of Six Sigma Purpose and Processes • Responsibilities of all Six Sigma roles during the life of a project	DEFINE • Reasons for the project selection • Defining customer needs/specifications • Understanding current process (rolled throughput) yield MEASURE • Basics of variation and Six Sigma Scales • Stratification and Basic Data Collection and Display • Flow Chart, Value Add Analysis • Pareto, Histogram, Bar & Pie Charts • Other measurement tools as needed ANALYZE • Control Charts (introduction to purpose, uses) • Cause and Effect Analysis and Verification • Other analysis tools as needed IMPROVE • Generating and Selecting Countermeasures • Action Planning • Other idea generating tools as needed IMPLEMENT • Planning tools as needed CONTROL • Project Scorecard • Process Control Plan

Ongoing Project Team Self-Assessment

In reality, project reviews occur every time a Six Sigma team meets. The team *constantly* must assess its own:

Process – How well is the team working? Is the DMAIIC process being followed? Are the right problem solving tools being used correctly?

Product – Are the tasks and deliverables getting done on schedule and within budget? What have we learned about our problem? How close are we to finding and implementing the solution?

Monthly Project Reviews

Regularly (monthly in a typical Six Sigma project), the Master Black Belt (or the external consultant) should meet with each project team. At the review meeting, the project team (NOT the Black Belt) answers the following standard review questions:

- What did we say we were going to do?
- What did we actually do?
- If we didn't do what we said we were going to do, why not?
- What are we going to do either to get back on track or follow a new track?
- What did we learn?
- What do we need in order to do better during the next month?

Intro

Ready ?

6 Months

Project

Long Haul

DMAIIC

Tools

R & R

The review meeting is more like a self-assessment report. The role of the reviewer is to ensure that:

- The team is using data, that supports what's being said.
- The DMAIIC process is being rigorously and properly used.
- The right problem solving tools are being used correctly.
- There are no technical errors, either in the application or in the interpretation of the tools.
- The project plan remains realistic, but aggressive.

The reviews also serve other critical, sometimes less tangible, purposes:

- To communicate/reinforce organizational priorities.
- To recognize, praise, reinforce
- To communicate emerging issues/priorities.
- To gain insight into the climate of team activities.
- To identify future needs such as resources, training, and follow-up.
- To reinforce expectations about performance.

Monthly Program Reviews

Based upon the monthly project team reviews, the Champion(s), Master Black Belt (or external consultant), and Black Belts should meet to assess the effectiveness of four program elements:

The Training	• Are team members confident and competent in their project work? • Are there topics that are creating confusion across project teams?
Team Leadership	• Are any of the Black or Green Belts in over his or her head? • Are the teams responding positively to all of the "belts."
The Project Teams	• Do we have the right people? • Are all of the players delivering what they are supposed to?
Support Systems	• Are the resources being provided? • Is leadership making the necessary decisions to keep the project moving forward?

12. Executive Education and Selection of Round 2 Projects, Black Belts, and Green Belts – Session #2 (1½ Days)

This one-and a-half day session combines a review of lessons learned from the first few months of project work with preparation for the second round of projects.

Champions report:

- Cross functional and/or systemic issues that have surfaced during projects and slowed their progress.

- The level of motivation evident in the project teams.

- Any recommended organizational changes (e.g. incentives to reward project teams for extraordinary efforts and results) that would accelerate project progress for the remainder of the first round and beyond.

Design for Six Sigma

First round projects generally deal with improvements to current processes. Later projects (under the leadership of more experienced Black Belts or Master Black Belts) apply the DMEDVI process to new processes and products. This session introduces the Executive Team to the basics of DFSS.

- Introduction to the DMEDVI (Define, Measure, Explore, Design, Validate, Implement) process.

- Gathering and understanding customer needs.

- Overview of QFD (Quality Function Deployment).

Selection of Round Two Projects, Black Belts, and Green Belts

In order for the Six Sigma implementation process to move ahead without interruption the Executive Team and Champions must select the next group of projects and the people who will lead them. For Round Two there are three classifications of projects:

1. *Introductory Black Belt Projects* – These are the "training ground" projects used to build the competence and confidence of newly appointed and trained Black Belts.

   Criteria: Same as first-round projects.

Intro

Ready ?

6 Months

Project

Long Haul

DMAIIC

Tools

R & R

2. *Advanced Black Belt Projects* – More complex projects (larger scale, multi-process, multiple facility) including DFSS applications for Black Belts who already have an introductory project "under their belt."

   Criteria: More sophisticated and even higher returns than the first-round projects.

3. *Green Belt Projects* – The less complex projects (often yielding surprisingly large savings) that can now be led by Green Belts who've been trained and mentored by Black Belts during the first round of projects.

   Criteria: Projects must have a significant impact on the Key Performance Indicators (KPI's) of the business unit and the process measures of the department or function.

> ### 19. 1st Round Project and Program Review; Communication of Results to the Organization (1 Day)

A Project and Program Review for all of the first-round project teams should be scheduled for the same day and should be led by the Champions. It should also directly involve the Executive Team, all of the "belts," and the project team members. In this review, you are looking for what Dr. Noriaki Kano, one of Japan's thought-leaders in Quality Improvement, calls "synthesis." This simply means that you know not only that you've reached your goals, but what you did to achieve them. This is where real learning occurs AND makes it possible to apply those lessons to other projects.

The Project Review (1/2 Day)
The Questions for each Project Team:

Business Results	Project Execution
❑ Was the targeted improvement in the KPI achieved? ❑ What was the ROI of the project? ❑ What was the total direct and indirect impact on the company or business unit profitability? ❑ What was the impact on core business processes? ❑ Was there a measurable improvement in customer satisfaction? Was the problem well-defined?	❑ Was the root cause identified using sound analysis of data and experience? ❑ Did the solution work? Is it working? How can the gain be held? How can it be replicated in other parts of the organization? ❑ Were the project deliverables produced on time? Were there foreseeable and avoidable project delays? ❑ Was the DMAIIC model followed from start to finish? ❑ Was the Project Scorecard complete and supported by the necessary documentation? ❑ Did the team work well as measured by: • Attendance at meetings. • Turnover within the team. • The average ratings on the team assessment form.

Intro
Ready ?
6 Months
Project
Long Haul
DMAIIC
Tools
R & R

The Design

To maximize the organizational learning from the Final Project Review:

- Turn the review into a "learning event" that is part science fair and part "shareholders meeting."
- Hold all of the reviews on the same day in a room large enough to accommodate all of the project teams and as many guests as possible.
- Allow 30 minutes per project team – a 15-minute team presentation and 15 minutes of questions from the Executive Team, Champions and the other project teams.
- Videotape the presentations so that the teams can fine-tune their skills. Also use it as a communications vehicle (e.g. play the tape continuously in the cafeteria)

Executive Team...

In Six Sigma (and in the entire organization), your job is to continuously improve processes, profits and people. The project review focuses on all three elements; it is also a golden opportunity to reinforce and recognize the hard work of good people. Even when the Six Sigma process falls short, the message you must convey is:

"We will positively learn from this round of projects AND commit to working together to do better!"

The Program Review (1/2 Day)
The Questions

A Program Review must focus *equally* on *business results* and *program execution* across all of the projects.

Intro

Ready ?

6 Months

Project

Long Haul

DMAIC

Tools

R & R

Intro

Ready ?

6 Months

Project

Long Haul

DMAIIC

Tools

R & R

Business Results	Project Execution
❑ Was the targeted improvement in the KPI's achieved?	❑ Were the selected projects good choices?
❑ What was the range and average ROI of the projects?	❑ What was the attendance rate at the training sessions?
❑ What was the total direct and indirect impact on the company or business unit profitability?	❑ What percentage of the Black Belt and Green Belt candidates were successfully certified?
❑ What was the impact on core business processes?	❑ What percentage of the projects were completed within the allotted time?
❑ Was there a measurable improvement in customer satisfaction?	❑ What percentage of the Black Belts were able to devote 100% of their time to assigned projects?
	❑ What needs to change in the next round of projects?

Expert Advice:

Lesson #1 - *Begin the implementation process under competent leaders (external AND internal) with clearly defined roles and expectations.*

External Leadership

Virtually all (learned long ago not to use "all" or "none") of the companies that have successfully implemented Six Sigma have used external consultants or consulting firms. In Chapter Two we addressed the criteria that should be used when selecting the best consulting candidate. After that decision has been made, the role of your qualified consultant must then be tailored to support the major "players" as illustrated in the following table.

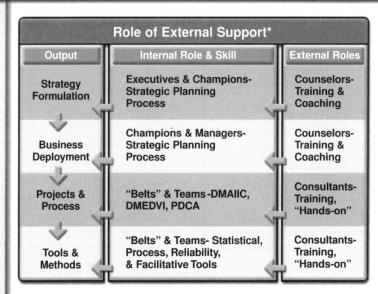

Role of External Support*		
Output	**Internal Role & Skill**	**External Roles**
Strategy Formulation	Executives & Champions-Strategic Planning Process	Counselors-Training & Coaching
Business Deployment	Champions & Managers-Strategic Planning Process	Counselors-Training & Coaching
Projects & Process	"Belts" & Teams -DMAIIC, DMEDVI, PDCA	Consultants-Training, "Hands-on"
Tools & Methods	"Belts" & Teams- Statistical, Process, Reliability, & Facilitative Tools	Consultants-Training, "Hands-on"

*Adapted from **Premier Performance Network** materials.

Internal Leadership
The Coaching Cascade

Training is obviously a huge component of Six Sigma, but for the senior leaders of the process (the Executive Team and Champions) *the coaching relationship* established with the consultant is even more critical. The consultant coaches leaders on:

- Key business decisions that may help or hinder Six Sigma implementation.
- Personal behavior that sends mixed messages.
- Ways to increase the acceptance of change.
- The proper use of Six Sigma process and tools.

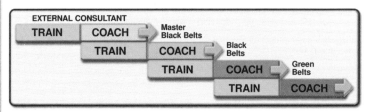

Each level (Master Black Belts through Green Belts) *MUST* establish this same coaching relationship with those they train and support in the projects. Otherwise, real learning can easily stop at the classroom door.

Accountability
Champions, Black Belts, Green Belts must be held accountable for what happens either under their direction or "on their watch." Functional managers must likewise be recognized or taken to task both for what they do and fail to do in support of projects in their area.

Zero Tolerance
NO ONE in the leadership structure can be excused from training. Everyone is watching for the first sign of wavering support. Besides, the training is actually necessary for Six Sigma leaders at all levels to fulfill their roles.

Lesson #2 – *Get all of the Six Sigma players out of the classroom and achieving concrete results as quickly as possible.*

The "learn-do" cycle must be built into any successful Six Sigma training design. So whether you're evaluating external training packages or designing your own, look for the following features:

- Every session MUST be a workshop (as opposed to a class) in which every person must produce a tangible output. Even in the case of a theoretical concept, each learner must practically apply it either to the Six Sigma project or to the process for which he or she is responsible.

- The overall program "training" plan should follow the 80/20 rule. The principle is "practice long" (80% of total project time) and "train short" (20% of total project time). For a typical 6 month Black Belt project this would mean:

Role/Time Commitment		Recommended Max. Classroom Time
Black Belts	(F/T)	5 Weeks
Green Belts	(P/T: 20%)	1 Week
Champions	(P/T: 40%)	2 Weeks
Project Team Members	(P/T: 10%)	2-3 Days

Intro

Ready ?

6 Months

Project

Long Haul

DMAIIC

Tools

R & R

Both the workload estimate and recommended class maximums are rules of thumb, not absolutes.

- The training must constantly be assessed to ensure that it's following this "learn-do" model. The Deployment/Program Champion is primarily responsible for this. This role is especially important since Six Sigma training is eventually delivered by a wide variety of people, ranging from seasoned external consultants to rookie Green Belts.

Warning #1 – *Don't be dishonest in your two-way communications flow; don't hype it...keep it visible and honest.*

- There must be from the beginning the practice of reporting the accurate status of all projects — warts and all. The difference lies in how the "off-target" projects are reported. They must be accompanied both by the diagnosis of what's not working and plan for corrective action to get back on track.

  The difference will lie in the approach that both the Champions and Executive team take to the "bad news". There is a simple leadership response that is virtually fool proof: "What do you need to be successful and what can we do to help to get you what you need?"

- Don't sell it as new; i.e. don't *talk* about the differences from past efforts. JUST CHANGE THE THINGS THAT MADE PREVIOUS APPROACHES FALL SHORT. Even if you announce the differences, experienced managers will still look for tangible signs of change, so what does the for mal pronouncement gain you? The strategy must be to keep moving forward, breaking through obstacles (not changing the project to avoid them), telling others how you did it and reporting results at every step...no more, no less.

Warning #2 – *Don't allow company leaders (especially the Executive Team) to disengage/or continue to be negative.*

As the Responsibility Flow Chart at the beginning of this chapter shows, leaders at all levels certainly play a VERY active *formal* role during the first six months of implementation. However, the rest of the organization is taking its cues from their *informal and personal behavior*. It's this behavior that reveals the underlying attitude toward the change effort.

There is a predictable distribution of attitudes towards any major change.

This may reflect the attitudes of organizations at large, but it's unacceptable within the management team. How do you move those who are negative/neutral to a positive, proactive position? The most successful Six Sigma implementations have been explicit about the "quid pro quo" for leaders.

Leaders must...	In order to get..
• Attend all of the required training. • Lead at least one Six Sigma project through the standard DMAIIC model. • Make the necessary resources available to support projects within the areas they manage. • Achieve significant improvement in their KPI's.	• Annual bonuses. • Promotions.

This approach strikes some as harsh and arbitrary. It's actually a very positive approach in that it focuses on providing clear reinforcement for those who contribute. This is much more effective than trying to "win-over" those who are either watching from the sidelines or digging in their heels.

Intro

Ready ?

6 Months

Project

Long Haul

DMAIIC

Tools

R & R

Intro

Ready ?

6 Months

Project

Long Haul

DMAIIc

Tools

R & R

Spillover Advice...

In this section, the key Lessons/Warnings from Six Sigma experts are included in the book. Other important Lessons/Warnings are listed below. They are well worth reading, but they are on the other side of an admittedly arbitrary line. Once in the e-book, just click on the icon next to any **Lesson** or **Warning #** to view it in its entirety.

Lesson #3 – *Establish a review & corrective action process–use it no matter what (CAP-Do).*

Lesson #4 – *Make a big deal out of integrating 6σ into regular management communication*

Lesson #5 – *Develop a highly visible scoreboard to track both the impact and the status of Six Sigma projects.*

Warning #3 – *Don't send conflicting messages about the priority of training*

Check List:

Have you...

☐ Selected first-round Six Sigma projects that created both significant financial impact and excitement?

☐ Selected, trained and supported talented and motivated Champions, Black Belts, Green Belts and Project Teams?

☐ Made significant progress toward 6σ performance in processes that matter the most to your customers?

☐ Made Six Sigma a highly visible part of your culture?

☐ Laid the groundwork to include Six Sigma performance in your reward and recognition system?

☐ Selected your next round of projects and "belts"?

☐ Assigned your first-round Black Belts and Green Belts to even more challenging projects with potentially higher paybacks?

Intro

Ready ?

6 Months

Project

Long Haul

DMAIIC

Tools

R & R

Chapter 4:
Doing a Project

Making a Six Sigma improvement project
a success

Purpose of this chapter:

To present a realistic picture of the process and product of a typical Six Sigma project team.

For senior executives this chapter...

- Provides an overview of the elements of a successful project team in order to make reviews more focused and meaningful.
- Translates the theory of Six Sigma into tangible actions and results.
- Illustrates the ongoing responsibilities of all of the major players in the Six Sigma process.
- Provides a realistic picture of the "life of a project team" that includes both the human and the technical challenges in the DMAIIC process.

For managers at all levels this chapter...

- Describes your leadership role (either as a team member or Green Belt) in detail and in a practical context.
- Illustrates the day-to-day role of Black Belts so that you can better support their work and tap their unique set of skills.
- Shows the DMAIIC process and primary tools in action.

The Big Picture:

Three Views of a Typical Six Sigma Project

This chapter draws three different pictures of Six Sigma projects:

1. *A Project Template*
2. *A Real-Life Project Case Study*
3. *Expert Advice*

Intro

Ready ?

6 Months

Project

Long Haul

DMAIIC

Tools

R & R

1. The way projects "should be" - *A Project Template*	The template starts with the product of each step in the Six Sigma process and then describes the steps, tools and responsibilities in a typical project.
2. The way projects are actually implemented - *A Project Case Study: Alphamega Refrigeration Corporation (A.R.C.)*	Follow an actual Six Sigma team from its initial meeting to project wrap-up. It's a very human look at how the process, tools and people produce results, both intended and unintended.
3. Bridging the gap between the project template and real life - *Expert Advice*	Experienced Six Sigma practitioners share their Lessons and Warnings about the "vital few" things to do and to avoid during your next project.

A Word of Caution: The project team template presented is meant to by *typical* and *not universal*. Adapt it to the culture and size of your company to make it workable, but *your* model must not violate ANY of the basic Six Sigma principles as outlined in Chapter 1. Likewise, the case study presented is not intended to be an exact replica of the generic template. It is one Six Sigma team's project experience from which we can all gain insights.

Manufacturing vs. Transactional Processes

The philosophy, problem solving process and tools of Six Sigma can be applied successfully to both the manufacturing and the service/administrative sides of the business. If you substitute the term, "transaction" (in a service process) for "part" (in a manufacturing process), the metrics of Six Sigma quality stay the same. This makes it possible to compare performance across very different functions, even when they appear to be "apples and oranges." Other key Six Sigma concepts like Critical to Quality (CTQ's) are equally important in transactional processes. The problem solving process itself remains remarkably consistent. There are some differences, however, in the "vital few" tools used in service vs. manufacturing processes. To understand the similarities and differences further, compare the "*RFP Case Examples*" (transactional process) included in the E-Book and the "*Alphamega Refrigeration Corporation*" case study (manufacturing process) that appears later in this chapter.

Responsibility Flow Chart

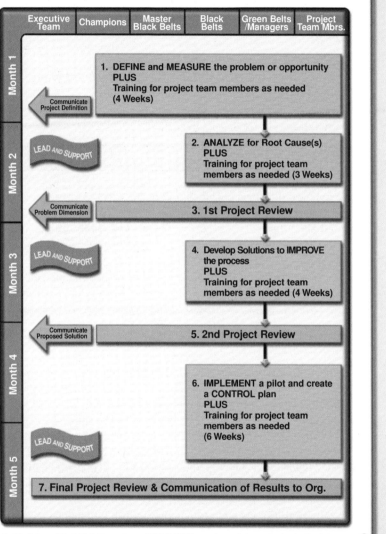

*   The Master Black Belt(s) are always "ON CALL" to review, advise and train the Black Belts and Project Teams in Six Sigma methods and processes. The Master Black Belt(s) can be called in at any step in the DMAIIC project process.

Intro

Ready ?

6 Months

Project

Long Haul

DMAIIC

Tools

R & R

Intro
Ready ?
6 Months
Project
Long Haul
DMAIIC
Tools
R & R

1. *DEFINE* and *MEASURE* the problem or opportunity (4 Weeks)

DEFINE

The Product:

A well-designed team with a well-defined project plan.

The Process:

Qualify – Approach – Outcomes – Stakeholders – Team Selection – Launch – Project Plan

On balancing team meetings with team work ...

Team meetings bog down when work that should be done between meetings becomes part of the agenda. Below are some distinctions that might help to prevent this.

At Meeting...
- Report progress
- Make recommendations
- Discuss options
- Make decisions
- Make assignments

Between Meetings...
- Collect information
- Gather and analyze data
- Conduct experiments
- Implement and monitor changes

IMPORTANT TASKS BEFORE THE PROJECT TEAM'S LAUNCH MEETING...

The *Lead Team,* a working group of the Executive Team, (sometimes called the *Implementation Team,* or *Steering Committee*) that also includes the Champions, works with representatives from Quality Assurance and Finance to analyze the data across all of the Improvement Focus Areas (See Chapter 3). They identify potential projects in each of the Focus Areas that will have the greatest bottom-line impact on achieving the business growth goals. The potential projects must also meet the Project Selection criteria presented in Chapter 1.

1. **"Qualify" the project and choose project approach**
   – Lead Team

   Before assigning resources and a team to a project, the Lead Team "qualifies" the project by analyzing historical data or by

Good historical data is very important; however, it's the importance of the problem that should always be the #1 criteria for selection.

collecting new data if needed, in order to determine:

- The *Complexity* of the system that surrounds the proposed problem.

- The *Financial Impact* of the proposed project.

- Whether the *Root Cause* of the problem/project is known or unknown.

The following grid shows which improvement approach to use based on these three factors:

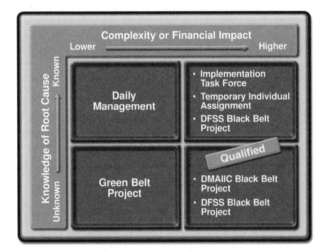

A "qualified" DMAIIC Black Belt project, therefore, has an *unknown root cause* combined with *significant complexity* OR a *sizable financial payback*.

Notice too, that a Design For Six Sigma (DFSS) Black Belt project appears in two quadrants. This occurs because projects requiring the development of entirely new products or process can spring from two situations:

- A *known root cause* in which the new product or process is designed to address a recognized, critical flaw. For example, redesigning a new child's safety seat, following recalls due to field failures of one key component, the handle lock assembly.

Intro

Ready ?

6 Months

Project

Long Haul

DMAIIC

Tools

R & R

Intro

Ready ?

6 Months

Project

Long Haul

DMAIIC

Tools

R & R

- An *unknown root cause* that's uncovered by a DMAIIC team may be impossible to solve given the present process or product design. For example, a DMAIIC team discovers that a process bottleneck can only be solved by a new, on-line process (a DFSS Project) because of an "impossibly" quick turnaround time demanded by a customer.

The fact that a proposal is "qualified" as a DMAIIC or a DFSS Black Belt project in no way diminishes the importance of the improvement approaches in the other quadrants. ALL of the approaches must be part of the "improvement portfolio" of a competitive organization.

2. **Define the outcome measure and target for the project –** Lead Team

Now that the Lead Team has decided that a project is qualified to move forward, it must communicate the need for change by quantifying the *performance gap*. This gap defines both the expectations of the team and the level of resources (people and capital) that should be allocated to finding a solution.

Required Performance (Customer-Defined)	–	*Current Performance* (Process-Defined)	=	*Outcome Measure/Target* (Financially-Defined)

3. **Identify the Stakeholders in the project –** Lead Team

Stakeholders in a project typically include customers of the process/product, the process owner/manager, associates in the process, internal and external suppliers to the process, and even shareholders. Why is it so important to identify the Stakeholders at this preliminary stage?

- At least some of the Stakeholders need to be represented on the project team.

- Stakeholder needs must be identified in order to identify a solution that will work for everyone involved in the problem.

Intro

Ready?

6 Months

Project

Long Haul

DMAIIC

Tools

R & R

4. **Create a charter for the project team** – Lead Team

    The most valuable contribution that the Lead Team can make to a project team is to provide clear direction and expectations. A <u>Team Charter</u> doesn't map the route for the project team, but it does provide the starting point, "geographic" boundaries and destination. It includes:

    - Project Objective
    - Process Boundaries
    - Limitations

    - Key Deliverables
    - Outside Resources
    - Indicator / Target

5. **Select the team** – Lead Team

    Finally, the Lead Team builds the Project Team itself by naming or soliciting:

    - *The Sponsor/Project Champion* who makes sure that the project has the resources and cross-functional support that it needs to succeed. Therefore, the Champion is the team member held most accountable by the Lead Team for the overall results of the project.

    - *The Project Leader* who manages the daily work of the entire team. In this template, the **Black Belt** plays this role, but it can also be the area manager, process owner or even a full-time project manager.

    - *The Team Members* who form the core work group (6-8 people) for the life of the project. Others with specialized knowledge (called "resources" or "subject-matter experts") work with the core group on an ad-hoc basis.

    > *Rules of the "Six Sigma" Road...*
    > • *Data Rules... Ego's Lose.*
    > • *Everybody. Every Mind. Every Time.*

    TEAM MEETING #1 – Project Launch

    Like any first meeting, the Launch Meeting of a Six Sigma project sets the tone and direction for the entire project.

    The following Launch Meeting agenda reflects a typical mix of building the team AND a solid implementation plan.

Intro

Ready ?

6 Months

Project

Long Haul

DMAIIC

Tools

R & R

Date: **Time:** *3 Hours*

In Attendance: *Process Owner/Manager, Project Champion/ Sponsor, Black Belt, Core Team Members, Master Black Belt*

Agenda:
1. *Review the Business Case of the project*
2. *Review, discussion and approval of the Team Charter*
3. *Develop team-behavior contract*
4. *Develop the Project Plan, including team information and project schedule.*

Assignments:

What	Who	By When
1. *Gather documentation on the current process*	*Black Belt*	*1 Week*
2. *Gather historical process data*	*Black Belt*	*1 Week*

Next Meeting: *In 1 Week*

The team uses a <u>Project Planning Worksheet</u> (or other project management templates provided in software packages such as Microsoft Project) to capture the key information about their team and the schedule for completing the major project milestones. This is the first stamp of project ownership by the team.

Example in the E-Book: *The Project Planning Worksheet for the project team formed to "Reduce the Number of Late Responses to Request for Proposals (RFP's)"*

MEASURE

The Product:
A project problem statement based upon a deep understanding of the current process and its capabilities.

The Process:
Current Process – Low-Hanging Fruit – Customer Requirements – Current Performance – Stratify Data – $ Benefit – Problem Statement

TEAM MEETING #2 – Defining the current process and harvesting the "low-hanging fruit."

Quickly create several versions of the current process. Choose the one that's the closest fit to reality as the discussion-starter.

The team builds upon the current documentation of the process to draw a realistic <u>Process Map (Responsibility Flow Chart)</u> of how the work actually gets done. Without a Process Map that everyone agrees is accurate, improvement to the process is impossible.

Example in the E-Book: *Process Map of the RFP Process*

If there are any team members who have not done any Process Mapping, be prepared to provide a tutorial that includes a number of simple process examples. The Process Map invariably uncovers "dumb stuff" (low-hanging fruit) that's become part of the accepted process. These obvious defects in the process include:

- Unclear requirements
- Non-value added activities
- Activities no longer needed.
- Bottlenecks/delays
- Unnecessary repetition

- Exception processing
- Manual vs. System processing
- Re-entry across multiple systems
- Multiple transfers

A <u>Process Deficiency Worksheet</u> can be used by the team to rate each "piece of low-hanging fruit" based on its cost, difficulty, negative impact, potential for rejection and amount of training required for implementation. Make the selected improvements as quickly as possible. This rapid and visible action creates savings, improved morale and a clearer picture of the fundamental process problems.

> *Another tool...*
> *a PFMEA*
> *(a Process-Failure-Mode & Effect-Analysis) to "torture-test the process.*

BETWEEN MEETINGS...Defining key customer requirements and CTQ's – Black Belt and Process Owner

Once the obvious improvements are made the team must decide which process measures to baseline and target for improvement. The place to start, as always, is with the customers of the process and their requirements. The Black Belt, working with the Process Owner, generally coordinates this process.

Intro

Ready ?

6 Months

Project

Long Haul

DMAIC

Tools

R & R

What's the best way to listen to the "voice of the customer"? There are many customer and market research methods available including Quality Function Deployment (QFD). Except for the largest scale projects, however, *interviews* and *customer complaint data* are the most widely used sources.

Kano's These "conversations" with the customer must result in an agreed-upon performance standard for the product of the process. For example, *"a complete response to an RFP within 5 working days of receipt of customer request."* This is what Dr. Kano calls "Requested Quality".

Turning Requirements into CTQ's

This will lead the team to a fundamental purpose of the Six Sigma model: to systematically improve the Critical-To-Quality Characteristics (CTQ's) IN a process in order to dramatically improve the products and services that come OUT of that process.

> A CTQ is...
> *What you manage and measure in the process that has a direct effect on the performance (or perceived performance) of the product or service in the hands of the customer. In some Six Sigma models, it is referred to as a "Key Process Variable" (KPV)*

Once again QFD can be used to identify CTQ's, but for the "average" team project a simpler option is presented below. This CTQ *Conversion Matrix* is a tool to capture three things that a team needs to know about *each major step* in their process:

1. The activities or variables that have a direct effect on one or more of the customer requirements.

2. The performance measure of those activities or variables.

3. The performance target for each of the measures.

Intro

Ready ?

6 Months

Project

Long Haul

DMAIIC

Tools

R & R

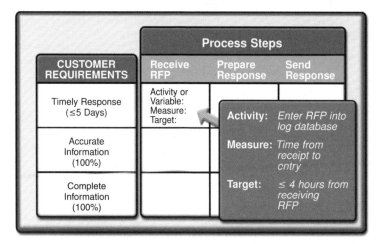

To keep the matrix to a manageable size, include only 3-6 "macro" steps and 2-4 customer requirements.

The Birth of a CTQ

The root of a CTQ is a measure of either an activity or variable that has a direct impact on a customer requirement.

> **Activity:** Enter RFP into log database
>
> **Measure:** Time from receipt to entry
>
> **CTQ:** Delays in entering the RFP in the log
>
> **Example in the E-Book:** *CTQ Conversion Matrix for the RFP process*

Another way...

Recognize that CTQ's identified at this stage, using this method, are based entirely on the experience and consensus of the team (including the Black Belt). A Designed Experiment could be done either at this point or in the "Improve" step when various solutions are tested and compared. As always, never use a tool that's more complex than the problem you're trying to solve. BUT… opinion-based decisions should ALWAYS be your second choice, AFTER it's decided that data is either impossible or unnecessary to collect.

Intro

Ready ?

6 Months

Project

Long Haul

DMAIIC

Tools

R & R

TEAM MEETING #3 – **Confirming CTQ's, process measures and data gathering assignments.**

The Black Belt, with the help of assigned team members, brings together all of the information related to CTQ's and recommendations for process measures. The team confirms and assigns responsibility for gathering data on CTQ's as well as:

- **Outcome Indicators** – Typically 1-3 measures that track the most critical customer requirements.

  Examples: Transaction accuracy; throughput yield; cycle time.

- **Process/Upstream Indicators** – These are the measures of activities or variables within the process sub-steps that have a significant impact on the outcome indicator(s), CTQ's and, therefore, on customer satisfaction.

  Example in the E-Book: *Process Indicator Matrix for the RFP process.*

If a process is fairly simple and everyone agrees on the relative importance of the measures, an unstructured discussion works fine. When this isn't the case, there's a range of tools that the team can use to rate the relative importance of the process measures.

1. **Nominal Group Technique (NGT)**
   NGT is a well-known consensus-building tool in which each team member independently ranks all of the potential process indicators. The lists are tallied and a "winner" emerges.

2. **Measures Matrix**
   A Measures Matrix allows the team to discuss and rate the impact of **ALL** of the potential Process/Upstream Indicators across **ALL** of the Outcome measures.

Don't leave the meeting without a list of assignments and answers to any *who, what, where, when* and *how* questions that data collectors might have. Use a simple, but complete Data Collection Template to ensure that this happens every time.

BETWEEN MEETINGS...Do a Gage R&R as needed; collect baseline data, including financial implications.
Black Belt and Team Members (often working in pairs)

A Data Collection Template addresses the *consistency of the collecting* of data, but not that of the *consistency of the data itself*. In a manufacturing process a <u>Gage R & R (Repeatability and Reproducibility) Study</u> can be done to confirm that the Process Measures will be accurate enough to rely on. In a Gage R&R study, samples are tested repeatedly:

- On the same equipment…for *repeatability*
- On different equipment…for *reproducibility*
- Over time…for *stability*

In a service application, the "human variable" has a larger impact on process measurement than in manufacturing. Therefore, assess the *repeatability, reproducibility* and *stability* of process perform-ance measures based on WHO is performing the measurement and the <u>operational definitions</u> that are being used.

Data Collection – Part I: Baselining and Benchmarking

Once it's clear that the data collecting systems are reliable, teams *typically* use the <u>Run Chart</u>, <u>Check Sheet</u>, <u>Pareto Chart</u>, <u>Control Chart</u> and <u>Histogram</u> *to collect and display* baseline data following this sequence:

1. To create a baseline, showing trends in process perform ance data, use a *Run Chart* to display Outcome quality data. Although it's not the norm, a *Control Chart* can be used as the first baselining tool. It provides the team with all the trend information of a Run Chart plus a view of the amount of process variation surrounding that trend.

   Example in the E-Book: *Run Chart on the Number of Late RFP Responses.*

   <u>Benchmarking</u> is another effective way to establish a per formance gap and target. In fact, finding a competitor with a world-class process capability may be the most motivating method of all.

> Some models have baselining in "Analyze" vs. "Measure." It doesn't matter as long as the data is sound.

Intro

Ready ?

6 Months

Project

Long Haul

DMAIC

Tools

R & R

Intro

Ready ?

6 Months

Project

Long Haul

DMAIIC

Tools

R & R

2. To collect and organize defect data on the CTQ's within the process, use a *Check Sheet*. This allows the team both to calculate an estimated Defects per Million Opportunities (DPMO) of the process and to prepare to stratify the data for deeper analysis.

   Example in the E-Book: *RFP Check Sheet that records process defects from among the CTQ's.*

3. To estimate the current performance of the process in Six Sigma terms *calculate the first-pass yield, defects per opportunity, DPMO, the longterm Sigma values.* The following example from an insurance operation illustrates these calculations.

Estimating current Sigma performance...

Step	Example	Value
1. Calculate total production volume	# of claims processed last month (+/- 2% of average monthly volume)	4,552
2. Calculate the # of 1st quality products	# of claims forms examined and found to be defect-free	3,552
3. Calculate 1st past yield (Step 2/Step1)	3552 defect-free claims forms out of 4552 forms processed	.7803
4. Calculate the defect rate (1.00-Step 3)	1000 out of 4552 claims forms found to have defects	.2197
5. Determine the # of CTO's in the process	The number of defect opportunities in the claims process that directly impact customer requirements	12
6. Calculate the defects per opportunity (Step 4/Step5)	The average claims defect rate across all CTQ's	.0183
7. Calculate the DPMO (Step 6 x 1 Million)	The number of defects found in 1 million opportunities if the process performs at its current quality level	18,307
8. Estimate the Long-Term Sigma value (using the Step 7 value and the Sigma Conversion Chart in Chapter 7)	The predicted capability of the current claims process in Six Sigma terms *over the long term* This figure already reflects the 1.5 Sigma shift in the centering of a process that typically occurs over time.	3.55σ

Example in the E-Book: *Calculation of the first-pass yield, defects per opportunity, DPMO, the short-term Sigma and the long-term Sigma values for the RFP process over the last 7 months.*

Data Collection – Part II: Stratifying The Data

A team classifies and separates data into groups in order to identify the most significant contributors to the performance gap exposed in the baseline data.

1. Use a *Pareto Chart* to further break down the "vital few" categories from the Check Sheet in Step 2 above.

   Example in the E-Book: *Pareto Chart of the "Reasons for Late RFP Responses"*

   While a Pareto Chart displays stratification by categories, the team also has to create a picture of the variation that exists in the process. ***THE REDUCTION OF THIS VARIATION IS THE FUNDAMENTAL PURPOSE OF THE DMAIIC PROCESS.*** The *Histogram* and the *Control Chart* are the tools of choice.

   > The SHAPE of the Histogram also shows whether the process has multiple distributions within it.

2. Use a *Histogram* to first show the centering and the spread within the entire output (population) of the process. By adding the specifications (the voice of the customer requirements) to the Histogram, the <u>Process Capability</u> can then be calculated answering the team question:

   > *"Can our process meet agreed upon customer requirements?"*

3. Use a *Control Chart* to show the centering and spread among *samples* from the process. While the Histogram shows the *capability* of the team's process, the Control Chart reveals the *stability* of the process. It answers:

   > *"Can our process produce consistent results?"*

Example in the E-Book: *Bar Chart of the "# of days RFP responses are late" and Histogram of the "Days to Prepare RFP Responses*

Example in the E-Book: *Control Chart of the "Days to Prepare RFP Responses"*

The Black belt or process owner gather all of the data and sit down with the Finance Department to identify the costs associated with the current process capability. The benefits of *dramatic* process improvement can then be quantified and presented to the team.

TEAM MEETING #4 – Interpreting the data, developing the problem statement, and starting the Project Scorecard.

Throughout the data collection process the Black Belt either collects the data or works closely with team members who have received that assignment. In either case, those responsible present the data at the meeting along with their interpretation. Once the team agrees that both the data and the conclusions are valid, they must then agree on a problem statement that:

- States clearly how the problem affects the business.

- Is stated in quantifiable, measurable terms.

- Ensures that the size and scope of the problem make it solvable.

In complex problems it may be necessary to use a tool such as the Affinity Diagram to organize the facts, observations and opinions of the team. The summary cards ("headers") can then be blended into a final problem statement. It is then recorded on the Project Scorecard along with the relevant data and project information.

> Don't include:
> - Possible causes
> - Possible solutions
> - Blame for a person or group.

Example in the E-Book: *Project Scorecard, "RFP's Responses Not Sent On Time Project Scorecard"*

Intro

Ready ?

6 Months

Project

Long Haul

DMAIIC

Tools

R & R

2. *ANALYZE* for Root Cause(s) (3 Weeks)

ANALYZE

The Product:
Root Cause(s) of the problem validated by facts.

The Process:
Hypothesize – Gather Data– Determine and Validate Root Causes

 TEAM MEETING #5 (or included in the agenda of Meeting #4) – Developing cause and effect hypotheses and cause investigation plans.

There's a natural flow between the *Measure* and *Analyze* phases since the act of collecting data invariably uncovers clues to cause and effect relationships. In the meeting, the team reviews all of the data collected to this point. What is it saying about the CTQ's?

If the problem is *cycle time* related (like the RFP example), ask:

- What percentage of the process steps adds value to the product or service?
- What did we uncover in our "low-hanging-fruit" activities? What were the deeper problems and process deficiencies?
- What steps in the process likely hold the root cause? Where are the processing bottlenecks? At which process steps are "products" piling up? Where should we dig deeper?
- Who should we talk to who's an expert in that part of the process? Are there process records that can "speak to us"?

If the problem is *defect* related (like the A.R.C. example), use the same "digging deeper" questions as in a cycle-time problem, but start by asking:

- Is there any special cause variation (unusual, explainable process changes/events) evident in the data?

The team agrees upon a plan and assignments to dig deeper into specific process steps and/or inputs to confirm that they are or are not root causes of the problem.

Cause and Effect analysis begins with experience-based guesses and progresses toward data-based analysis.

BETWEEN MEETINGS... Gather Causal Data –
Black Belt and Team Members

The Black Belt and team members go where the facts and experience are: the process documentation, data and location.

For cycle time related problems use the Process Maps and iden-
tified problem areas that the team has already established to:

- Begin playing with improvement scenarios, or even
  conduct small "experiments." Estimate the potential time
  savings if something were changed in the process. Look
  at benchmarks of the process done differently elsewhere.

For defect related problems:

- Review defect data such as Failure Analysis Reports and
  Material Review Board (MRB) reports.Talk to operators/
  associates in the process about the team's root cause
  theories.

TEAM MEETING #6 & #7 – Determining the Root
Causes and making plans to validate them.

Meeting #6 is actually a continuation of data gathering in that it's a
compilation of the data and observations collected by the Black Belt
and team members. Two meetings are set aside for this step because
the process normally takes longer than expected. This is especially
true, if meetings are the typical 1-2 hours in length. To organize all
of the causal information in preparation for deeper analysis, teams
use two core tools: The Affinity Diagram and the Cause & Effect
(Fishbone) Diagram.

1. Use the Affinity Diagram to first generate the "master list"
   of everything the team knows about the causes of the problem. The Affinity process enables the team to then organize
   this "knowledge-dump" into meaningful cause categories.

2. Use the cause categories created in the Affinity as the start
   ing point for the Cause & Effect (Fishbone) Diagram.
   Apply the 5 Why's technique to the causes as you add
   more and more detailed, "bones" to the Fishbone Chart.
   Stop generating deeper causes when they go beyond the

> Create a
> "virtual" Six Sigma
> team by tapping
> the experience of
> the "process-
> knowledge
> workers."

reasonable control of the team or project stakeholders.

Ultimately the team has three decisions to make:

1. When to stop asking "why?"
2. What the most likely root cause is.
3. How to validate the team's choice of root cause(s).

The Black Belt must lead the analysis AND prepare team members to do it the next time.

When the Cause & Effect analysis produces just one root cause "candidate," the rest of the process is pretty straightforward – develop solutions, run a pilot implementation and measure the impact on the Outcome Indicator. The "validation" happens naturally as part of the PDCA process.

But when there's the possibility that *multiple root causes* (either independent or interacting) need to be compared, a variety of "experimental" tools need to be considered. The Black Belt recommends the proper design and leads the execution of the experiment.

BETWEEN MEETINGS... Validate causes – Black Belt with team member assistance

The simplest way to compare the range of tools and analytical methods that are available is with a few scenarios that reflect different combinations of possible causes.

Validate Causes

Situation: A machine applies a very thin latex backing on cloth. There are serious yield problems because of inconsistent latex coverage.

Scenario #1: One potential root cause; one experiment - A team decided that a lack of Standard Operating Procedures was the root cause of the latex-backing problem. They developed SOP's and implemented them on the 1st shift. They measured yield across shifts. There was a significant difference and they replicated the SOP's across the shifts.

...continued on next page

Intro

Ready ?

6 Months

Project

Long Haul

DMAIIC

Tools

R & R

Intro

Ready ?

6 Months

Project

Long Haul

DMAIIC

Tools

R & R

Validate Causes *(continued)*

Scenario #2: Multiple (two) root causes; repeated experiments using one cause (factor) at a time - There were two competing root causes: Line speed and latex viscosity. The team decided to use two **Scatter Diagrams to see the direction and strength of the relationship between each factor (cause) and latex coverage (effect)**. The Black Belt also ran Correlation Tests (e.g. Correlation Coefficient and Regression Analysis). Line speed was inconclusive, but Viscosity had a strong positive correlation with latex coverage.

Scenario #3: Multiple (five) root causes, repeated experiments using all five factors simultaneously - The team identified five potential causes: latex viscosity, line speed, pad temperature, cloth moisture level and nozzle air pressure. There was strong support for each cause, with most of the team betting on changes in the latex itself. The Black Belt did a Full Factorial Design of Experiment, including Analysis of Variance (ANOVA) using all five factors. The team was surprised that the experiment showed the real root cause was the pad temperature. It had an interaction with cloth moisture level. The team started out thinking that the problem was in the latex, but it was actually in the characteristics of the cloth itself.

3, 5. Project Reviews

TEAM PROJECT REVIEW MEETINGS – **Keeping project teams motivated and on track** – Monthly Reviews

The key to positive reviews can be summed up in two words: NO SURPRISES – for either those being reviewed or for the reviewers. The Six Sigma model prevents surprises in three ways:

Intro
Ready?
6 Months
Project
Long Haul
DMAIIC
Tools
R & R

1. **A standard review-meeting model** – Something as simple as a standard agenda can decrease the natural variation in style occurring from reviewer to reviewer. It also creates an accurate picture of the scale and scope of expectations.

Date: Monthly   **Time:** 1 hour

In Attendance: Process Owner/Manager, Project Champion/Sponsor, Black Belt, Core Team Members, Master Black Belt

Agenda: **Time (min)**

1. Team presents progress to date in solving the problem and in applying the DMAIIC process and tools 10-15
2. Team addresses any open action items 5
3. Reviewers ask questions based upon the DMAIIC Story Checkpoints 5-10
4. Team responds to questions 5-10
5. Team discusses next steps 10
6. Reviewers summarize review, feedback and action items 5
7. Assessment of review meeting 5

Assignments:

What	Who	By When
1. Corrective actions suggested by the reviewers	Manager, Black Belt or Team Member	1 month

Next Meeting: In 1 month

---

2. **A standard review item template** – The DMAIIC Story Checkpoints List essentially gives the team the "answer sheet for the test." It lists the core tools that should be used and the fundamental questions that must be answered at each step of the DMAIIC model.

3. **A constant communications link** – Of all the roles the Black Belt plays, none is more important than that of communications link. A Black Belt who is in weekly (even daily) touch with stakeholders is a powerful, and necessary addition to any formal reporting system.

4. Develop solutions to *IMPROVE* the process (4 Weeks)

IMPROVE

The Product:
A cost-effective action plan to eliminate or dramatically reduce the impact of the root cause.

The Process:
Breakthroughs – Practical Approaches – Cost/ Benefit – Future State – Performance Targets – Scorecards

TEAM MEETING #8 – Developing countermeasures

The team's challenge is to first expand its thinking to include possible breakthrough solutions and then quickly create some practical alternatives. The team can choose from some excellent, proven tools to get the job done:

- **Brainstorming** – Still the best way to "get the creative juices flowing."

- **Benchmarking** – Look for successful solutions both inside and outside your industry.

- **Affinity Diagram** – Let the breakthroughs emerge naturally.

The team should then pass EVERY seriously proposed countermeasure through standard screening criteria in order to choose one or more practical alternatives. This is important for two reasons:

1. It prevents untraditional approaches from being abandoned simply because they're different.

2. It places a high value on the ideas of every team member.

The team uses a *Countermeasure Selection Matrix* to systematically rate all of the alternatives and select the option that fares the best across all of the criteria.

> Black Belts must become "facilitators" so that the team can now assume the role of "solution expert."

Intro

Ready ?

6 Months

Project

Long Haul

DMAIC

Tools

R & R

Countermeasure Criteria

Effective:
- Will it solve all or part of the problem?
- Will it achieve the target for improvement?
- Has this been tried before?

Timely:
- How quickly will it work?
- How soon are the results needed?
- How long will the results last?

External customer oriented:
- Will it satisfy Key Customer Requirements (KCR's)?
- Will it improve service or product quality?

Feasible:
- Can this countermeasure be implemented?
- Is it practical?

Internal customer oriented:
- What is the cost benefit?

All criteria are created equal, BUT... "effectiveness must always be #1.

> **Example in the E-Book:** *Countermeasure Selection Matrix, "Solutions to the RFP Project's Root Cause"*

 BETWEEN MEETINGS... Do the cost/benefit analysis on the countermeasures – Black Belt

Following the selection of the countermeasures, the Black Belt works with Finance to estimate the investment needed to implement it. The difference between this cost estimate and the projected Internal and External Failure Costs of the problem, if it's unsolved, is the *Estimated Net Financial Benefit*.

> **Example in the E-Book:** *Cost/Benefit Analysis, "Implementing the Countermeasures to the RFP Project's Root Cause"*

Intro
Ready ?
6 Months
Project
Long Haul
DMAIIC
Tools
R & R

DON'T ask for feedback on the proposed process if you're not prepared to **listen**, **learn**, and **let go**.

TEAM MEETING #9 – Developing and documenting the action plan

Assuming that the financial return justifies their countermeasure, the team must describe the redesigned process, its new performance targets and the action plan to put it in place.

The Process Map/Responsibility Flow Chart is the best tool to create a draft that can be circulated to the stakeholders in the process. It's so effective as a review document because it presents a complete picture of both the flow of activity and responsibilities.

Establishing Process/Upstream Indicators and Outcome Indicators for the proposed process, allows the team to set appropriate performance targets for each.

In a straightforward project, the team can generate a simple sequenced list of tasks and assignments – the Action Plan. A simple, but invaluable, extra step is to "mistake-proof" the plan by doing some contingency planning using a <u>Process-Decision-Program-Chart (*PDPC*)</u>.

Finally, the team records the major tasks (6-10 steps) of the action plan on the Project Scorecard. The Scorecard becomes the team's primary reference document for itself and the rest of the organization.

> **Example in the E-Book:** *Project Scorecard, "Action Plan to Address the RFP Project's Root Cause"*

BETWEEN MEETINGS... Develop a detailed project plan, as needed – Black Belt and/or Project Manager

For more complex (or risky) projects, teams use the full array of project management tools including <u>GANTT Charts</u> and <u>Activity Network Diagrams (AND)</u>, based upon the leading Project Management Software.

Intro

Ready ?

6 Months

Project

Long Haul

DMAIIC

Tools

R & R

6. *IMPLEMENT* a pilot and create a CONTROL plan (6 Weeks)

IMPLEMENT

The Product:
An implemented change process that follows a well thought out action plan.

The Process:
Gain Approval to Implement – Train – Execute– Measure Results – Develop Control Methods – Manage Change

 TEAM MEETING #10 – Getting the action plan approved

One of the major benefits of using the DMAIIC model is that the team has documented everything that it needs for a compelling presentation of its plan to the Lead Team.

Date:　　　　　　　　　　　　　　　**Time:** *1 hour*

In Attendance: *Lead Team, Process Owner/Manager, Project Champion/ Sponsor, Black Belt, Core Team Members, Master Black Belt*

Agenda:
1. *Present Project Scorecard and supporting data.*
2. *Summarize details of required resources*
3. *Specify the targeted results (how much & when).*

Next Meeting: *In 1 month*

> Whenever possible, use the tools and techniques of Six Sigma in the presentation itself.

 BETWEEN MEETINGS... Introduce the changes into the organization – Black Belt and/or Project Manager

The team must treat any improvement as a managed change process in which real people have to learn and practice new habits and skills. There are five standard actions the team must commit to with EVERY implementation:

1. **Train** people thoroughly in the new process.

2. **Communicate** the plan, then stop and listen.

3. **Lead** the change with integrity and guts.

4. **Reinforce** those who are being asked to change.

5. **Measure** and feedback the results of the plan.

CONTROL

The Product:
A Process for Maintaining Improvements

The Process:
Report Scorecard Data – Create Process Control Plan –
P-D-C-A Process – Identify Replication Opportunities –
Develop Future Plans

TEAM MEETING #11 – Checking the results of the pilot implementation and holding the gains.

Typically after a 3-4 week pilot implementation of the process changes, the team meets to assess their plan and develop a plan for continued monitoring of the new process. They first review their scorecard results. Did the plan have its planned impact? Did the results occur because of the actions taken or because of other changes in the system?

Invariably, the team agrees upon some adjustments to the original plan based on pilot results. The team incorporates these changes into the Process Control Plan using the Process Control Template. The template includes three essential components:

1. Original and revised Responsibility Flow Charts.

2. The new measures and the system to monitor them.

3. Responses to poor performance in the measures.

Examples in the E-Book: *Project Scorecard Results and Process Control Plan for "Action Plan to Address the RFP Project's Root Cause"*

Examples in the E-Book: *Original and revised Responsibility Flow Charts for "Action Plan to Address the RFP Project's Root Cause"*

*BETWEEN MEETINGS...*Fine tuning and future planning – Black Belt

A big part of the power of Six Sigma is the quality of the documentation that accompanies the diagnosis, cure and control of a problem. The Black Belt must ensure that the documentation that supports the project scorecard is complete and cler to the rest of the organization. Finally, the Black Belt must confirm that the full-scale implementation plan is indeed workable and effective.

> ### 7. Final Project Review and Communication of Results to the Organization

TEAM MEETING #12 – Wrapping up the project and the team.

This final team meeting serves two purposes: the team must process its own project experience and plan its final review presentation.

The Team Review – What did we learn about...	
• The tools?	• DMAIIC?
• Team leadership?	• Teamwork?
• Team Roles?	• Communications?
• Data collection & analysis	• Project management?

Many companies leverage the power of final reviews by combining the reviews of all of the teams completing their projects around the same time. A detailed design of this type of review session can be found in Chapter Three.

Date: *17 weeks from project start*   **Time:** *1 hour*
In Attendance: *Lead Team, Process Owner/Manager, Project Champion /Sponsor, Black Belt, Core Team Members, Master Black Belt*
Agenda:
1. Present Project Scorecard results.	*4. Present team learnings.*
	5. Reviewer questions.
2. Present final control plan.	*6. Recognition of the team.*
3. Identify any additional opportunities.	

Assignments:
What	Who	By When
Monitor control plan	*Black Belt*	*6-12 months*

Next Meeting: *At the discretion of the Black Belt*

Intro

Ready ?

6 Months

Project

Long Haul

DMAIIC

Tools

R & R

Intro

Ready ?

6 Months

Project

Long Haul

DMAIIC

Tools

R & R

A Six Sigma Case Study:

Alphamega Refrigeration Corporation

The following Six Sigma project case study is based on actual conditions, processes, activities, and data as reported by a major international manufacturer. The name of the company, plant locations, names of the participants, and other proprietary information, situations, and data have been altered at the company's request. All costs and savings are described in U.S. dollars.

It was July 1998. Alphamega Refrigeration Corporation, a Camden, NJ-based manufacturer of equipment for the supermarket and food service industries with $475 million in sales, had begun to see its once significant market share eroding. In survey after survey, customers had told them the same thing: ARC's products were too expensive to purchase and maintain. Internal production costs at its 14 plants—especially some staggering figures for rework and warranty repairs—had kept Alphamega from pricing as aggressively as they had needed to meet growing global competition.

At the end of July, in an effort to return the company to a competitive position in the marketplace, Alphamega hired new CEO, Frida Jorgenson. During the last quarter of 1998, she and her staff did some extensive research, scenario building, and benchmarking. They decided they had only two choices: close plants and lay off workers, or decrease costs through a corporate-wide commitment to Six Sigma management.

So, on January 4, 1999—with a week of executive education, team building, and training—Alphamega Refrigeration began its life as a Six Sigma company. On May 3, 1999, after four months of planning and corporate-level data analysis, Alphamega's first Six Sigma project was born.

This is the story of that project.

Intro

Ready ?

6 Months

Project

Long Haul

DMAIC

Tools

R & R

May 3, 1999 — *Six Sigma Project Kickoff Meeting*
Alphamega Condenser Plant – Santos, Brazil

Seven people sat in the conference room nervously awaiting the arrival of plant manager, Carlos Aguiar:

- Maria Pinheiro, manager, line four, second shift
- Jorge Cabral, QA manager
- Jonas Rezendes, manager, line one, second shift
- Joao Souza, production inspector, first shift
- Joao Alcantara, production engineer
- Miguel Calheiros, shift manager, second shift
- Bernice Diaz, shift manager, first shift

They spoke quietly among themselves. None of them knew why they were there, but they each had their theories, not one of them good.

> *"During the previous couple of months, there had been talk of layoffs. Until a year and a half ago, I'd had a great line job at Ford's Sao Paulo engine plant. As I sat waiting that day, I was wondering if I'd made the right choice to hire on into management at ARC.*

Line manager
(through an interpreter)

As Carlos Aguiar and two other men entered the room, the group shifted awkwardly in their seats. None of them knew who the second man was, but they all knew the third man, Alvaro Andrade, Alphamega's vice president of Brazilian operations. This definitely was going to be something big.

By the end of the morning, Aguiar, Andrade, and newly hired Black Belt Gilvam Machado had been able to convince the seven their jobs were secure. After lunch, they focused on the real task at hand—kicking off the largest cost reduction project in the company's history.

> *"I met Alvaro Andrade at a conference when I was still a Green Belt at Motorola in Campinas. Three months ago—after he'd become this project's Champion—he hired me to become a Black Belt for Alphamega Santos. I was glad for my experience at Motorola. It cut almost a month off my Black Belt training in the states."*

Gil Machado
Newly hired Six Sigma Black Belt, ARC Santos

Plant Manager Aguiar and VP Andrade quickly made the case for selecting Santos as the site for ARC's first Six Sigma effort. They drew the group's attention to a chart displaying two Pareto diagrams previously developed by a project selection team at ARC headquarters in Camden.

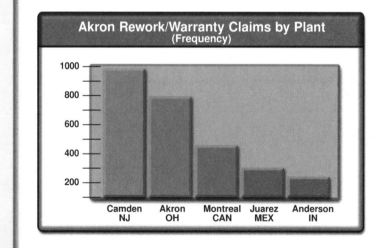

© *2001 Brassard & Ritter, LLC*

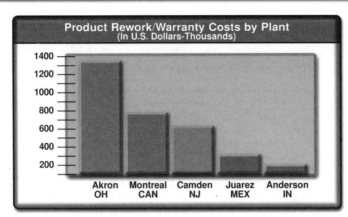

Product Rework/Warranty Costs by Plant
(In U.S. Dollars-Thousands)

The VP of Operations stressed what these charts had confirmed to the selection team—as a company, rework and warranty claims were killing them. The total rework cost for Alphamega's five largest plants amounted to more than $2.9 million, or 1% of their combined sales output. Clearly, the most serious problem was at the Akron, Ohio, refrigerated display case assembly plant, where rework and warranty repair was costing more than 2% of total output.

With that, Black Belt Gil Machado stepped forward to display a third Pareto, prompting one team member to voice what was on everyone's mind:

"So this is where Santos comes in."

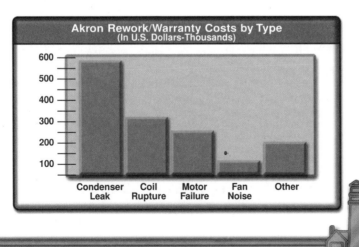

Akron Rework/Warranty Costs by Type
(In U.S. Dollars-Thousands)

They all knew that every condenser used in Akron was made right there in Santos. Now they also knew that their leaking condensers were costing Akron an incredible $580K in pre- and post-sale repairs. That concern was written on each of their faces.

> *"Everyone was worried and a bit embarrassed by the size and importance of the project. I told them Akron only wanted two things from us—units that hold up under the 135% pressure test and zero warranty claims for condenser leaks. We joked about calling ourselves 'Team Leaks.' I guess the name just stuck."*
>
> **Carlos Aguiar**
> *Plant Manager, Team Leaks Project Leader*

To show Alphamega's solid corporate support, and ensure top-to-bottom involvement of the Santos workforce, Aguiar and Machado ended the kickoff meeting by joining VP Andrade in unveiling the Team Leaks "Share the Savings" plan. If they were as successful as projected, Alphamega Refrigeration Corporation would share $58K (10% of anticipated annual savings of $580K) with its Santos plant management and workers.

Week 3 — May 17, 1999
As requested, each Team Leaks member spent the two weeks after the kickoff meeting reviewing the Santos condenser manufacturing process in action looking for factors that might contribute to head leaks. Under Black Belt Machado's watchful eye, Carlos Aguiar led the group through an initial analysis of their findings using a Cause and Effect Diagram. (See top of next page.)

From his Black Belt training, Gil Machado recognized that the team would now need to determine which variable, or combination of variables, has the most impact on "leaky condensers." He explained to them how a Design of Experiments (DOE) procedure could give them the answers they were looking for in a few months.

Intro

Ready ?

6 Months

Project

Long Haul

DMAIIC

Tools

R & R

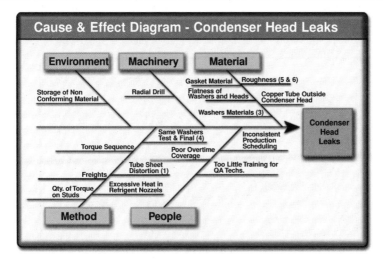

Cause & Effect Diagram - Condenser Head Leaks

However, he also knew the team would still have to operate in a very real world of production requirements, cost restrictions, and time limitations. To limit the scope of the experiment, the team would have to:

- Find a more precise measure than "Leak/No Leak."

- Limit the number of DOE variables to be tested.

Machado conferred with team leader Aguiar during the break, then asked the group to think about these two problems during the following week and come to the next meeting with some ideas and possible solutions.

Week 4 — May 24, 1999

Only the second shift manager and the QA manager came prepared with a suggestion of what to measure for the DOE. They'd met at the end of the first shift on Friday to review the manufacturing process from their two distinct perspectives. The team agreed that their idea to measure "Torque Loss" on the bolts attaching the condenser heads was a good one—without torque loss there would be no leaks and even tiny variations could be measured. To narrow down the list of "heavy hitters," the group decided to tap into the

Intro

Ready ?

6 Months

Project

Long Haul

DMAIC

Tools

R & R

Intro

Ready ?

6 Months

Project

Long Haul

DMAIIC

Tools

R & R

expertise and intuition found right there on their team and in the Santos workforce.

> *"Senhor Aguiar asked me and three other line leaders to brainstorm with him and his team for a couple of hours. They had a list of things that lead to condenser leaks and wanted to know which ones we thought would make the biggest difference. It was pretty simple. You'd think they'd have known. Well, at least they asked."*

Line Leader,
Line Six, First Shift (through an interpreter.)

That afternoon, although they were still unclear as to just what a Design of Experiments was and how it would help them solve the condenser-leak problem, Team Leaks and their guests from the factory floor came up with five factors to use in the process:

- **Distortion –** A device called a "Strong Back" was used to control distortion. Units with and without Strong Back would be tested.

- **Torque Sequence –** Specs called for bolts to be torqued in a specific, but not commonly followed, sequence. Spec sequence and a "common" sequence would be used.

- **Washer Material –** Test would include current weight (light) vs. strong weight (medium) washers.

- **Washer Replacement –** After hydrostatic tests (all units), final head gaskets were often replaced, using washers from the original gaskets. Fearing function loss from pre-torqued (deformed) used washers, both new and used washers would be tested.

- **Torque Quantity** – After hydrostatic tests, bolts are tightened one last time. Tests would be at 65 lb/ft torque and 75 lb/ft torque.

The brainstorming session went longer than planned, the meeting adjourned before everything on the agenda could be covered. In their post-meeting discussion, both Carlos and Gil were concerned, but for different reasons.

Aguiar was upset because they hadn't laid out the action plan—a duty roster and schedule—for the upcoming Design of Experiments. As the plant manager and team leader, he was feeling pressure from the home office to keep this critical Six Sigma project on track.

Machado, the Black Belt, on the other hand, was worried that the team was being overwhelmed with new and confusing information. He'd seen that familiar "deer in the headlights" look on the faces of several team members that afternoon. They needed DOE and other skills training, and quickly, to keep the project from floundering.

With the warning, "Camden is breathing down our necks," Carlos convinced Gil to wait a couple of weeks for the training so that the team could get the Action Plan up and running. Before going home for the night, he issued a memo announcing Gil's one-day training session for June 1 and a special Action Plan meeting on May 26th, just two days away. Carlos Aguiar went home happy that night— Team Leaks was back on track.

Week 4 — May 26, 1999
Special Team Leaks DOE Action Plan Meeting

After the last marathon session, team leader Aguiar was determined to keep this meeting brief. As promised, everyone brought updated calendars and Gil Machado brought a template for the DOE action plan. They were done in 45 minutes as planned. The team left the meeting dazed by the aggressive schedule.

Intro

Ready ?

6 Months

Project

Long Haul

DMAIC

Tools

R & R

Intro

Ready ?

6 Months

Project

Long Haul

DMAIIC

Tools

R & R

Action Plan for Design of Experiments (DOE)

#	Action	Who	Start	Finish
1	DOE definition	Team Leaks	17-May-99	19-May-99
2	Graph Akron leak claims	J.Cabral	30-Jun-99	Ongoing
3	DOE training session	G. Machado/Tm.	1-Jun-99	1-Jun-99
4	Flowchart for DOE	G. Machado	3-Jun-99	10-Jun-99
5	"Strong Back" for DOE	S. Aguiar	11-Jun-99	11-Jun-99
6	"Special washers" for DOE	M. Calheiros	10-Jun-99	17-Jun-99
7	Collect DOE information	J. Cabral	4-Jun-99	30-Jul-99
8	Collect info from Akron plant	V. Stepcik	24-Jun-99	19-Aug-99
9	DOE evaluation	Aguiar/Machado	23-Aug-99	25-Aug-99
10	Final actions	Team Leaks	26-Aug-99	24-Sep-99

Week 10 — July 9, 1999
Project Review Meeting

Every other Friday, just before second shift, Team Leaks met for a 30-minute project review. This was the fifth such update and there was tension in the air. Three people hadn't shown and everyone was starting to feel uncomfortable with the extra work that came from being on the team.

Earlier, the second-shift manager had called Gil Machado—he and his two line managers would not be able to make the meeting. He told Gil he was trying to appease the assistant plant manager who'd been coming down hard on the second shift for excessive overtime. Gil reminded the shift manager of his responsibility to the critical project, but couldn't convince him to change his mind. He promised Gil that he and his two line managers would deliver on all assigned action items, "but I don't think it'll be a big deal if the three of us miss a couple of reviews."

"Get me those three!"

That was all Carlos Aguiar could manage after Gil told him what had happened. He left the room, slamming the door on his way out. The meeting was over before it had begun.

Intro

Ready ?

6 Months

Project

Long Haul

DMAIC

Tools

R & R

> "To be
> fair to the three second-shift guys,
> Carlos missed the last two reviews himself. I
> led the one on June 11th while he was at a plant
> manager's meeting in Camden. The last meeting he
> was leading a plant tour for our state senator
> and his entourage from
> Brazilia."

Gill Machado,
Team Leaks Black Belt

Week 17 — August 27, 1999
Special TL Project Review Meeting – DOE Results

Seven hectic weeks followed the July 9th "meeting that never was." The Design of Experiments, at first so intimidating to the group, had gone smoothly, despite the fact the plant was running at 110% capacity. They had Black Belt Gil Machado to thank for his well-timed skill-building sessions in DOE, Project Management, and Team Motivation. Now, they were ready to deal with the results.

Machado and team leader Aguiar were ready, too. Before displaying the Results Matrix on the meeting room flip chart, they reminded the team about the "givens" in the experiment:

- DOE Result = (Initial Torque) – (Final Torque)

- Torque = average of individual bolt measurements

- Positive (+) value = Torque Loss

- Negative (-) value = Torque Increase

Results Matrix - Design of Experiments (DOE)

Item/ Test	Strong Back	Torque Sequence	Washer Materials	Washers New/Used	Torque Qty	Frontal Head	Rear Head
1	No	Current	Current	Used	65	11.54	7.04
2	No	Adequate	Current	Used	65	4.3	6.13
3	No	Current	Current	New	65	16.63	12.40
4	No	Adequate	Current	New	65	15.36	9.77
9	No	Current	Reinforced	Used	65	21.00	20.40
10	No	Adequate	Reinforced	Used	65	9.31	4.31
11	No	Current	Reinforced	New	65	5.45	8.18
12	No	Adequate	Reinforced	New	65	14.09	9.54
17	Yes	Current	Current	Used	65	10.68	10.68

Item/ Test	Strong Back	Torque Sequence	Washer Materials	Washers New/Used	Torque Qty	Frontal Head	Rear Head
22	Yes	Adequate	Current	Used	75	-1.13	0.22
23	Yes	Current	Current	New	75	-1.36	2.50
24	Yes	Adequate	Current	New	75	12.72	9.00
29	Yes	Current	Reinforced	Used	75	1.13	1.20
30	Yes	Adequate	Reinforced	Used	75	12.04	13.63
31	Yes	Current	Reinforced	New	75	9.77	11.82
32	Yes	Adequate	Reinforced	New	75	8.40	5.9

NOTE:
The two DOE data tables on this and the next page have been shortened to conserve space.

"These managers off the floor aren't used to working with numbers all day like I am. You could see them glazing over more and more with each chart Carlos put up. In fact, he had his hands full keeping everyone focused on the analysis. These guys just wanted to talk about fixing the problem."

Production Engineer,
TL member (through interpreter)

DOE Analysis - Factorial Fit
Estimated Effects and Coefficients (Front Head Only)

Term	Effect	Std. Dev. Coeff.	Coeff.	T	P
Constant		9.720	1.603	6.06	0.001
Strong B	-11.007	-5.503	1.603	-3.43	0.014
Sequence	0.031	0.015	1.603	0.01	0.993
Material	-0.931	-0.465	1.603	-0.29	0.781
Washers	3.572	1.786	1.603	1.11	0.308
Qty Torq	3.992	1.996	1.603	1.24	0.260
Strong B*Sequence	2.782	1.391	1.603	0.87	0.419
Strong B*Material	0.613	0.307	1.603	0.19	0.855
Washers*Qty Torq	3.864	1.932	1.603	1.21	0.274

Term	Effect	Std. Dev. Coeff.	Coeff.	T	P
Strong B*Sequence*Washers	-1.731	-0.865	1.603	-0.54	0.609
Strong B*Sequence*Qty Torq	1.337	0.668	1.603	0.42	0.691
Strong B*Material*Washers	-3.132	-1.566	1.603	-0.98	0.366
Strong B*Material*Qty Torq	3.821	1.910	1.603	1.19	0.278
Strong B*Washers*Qty Torq	-0.714	-0.357	1.603	-0.22	0.831
Sequence*Material*Washers	-3.887	-1.943	1.603	-1.21	0.271
Sequence*Material*Qty Torq	-0.197	-0.098	1.603	-0.06	0.953
Sequence*Washers*Qty Torq	-1.189	-0.595	1.603	-0.37	0.723
Material*Washers*Qty Torq	5.559	2.780	1.603	1.73	0.134

Variance Analysis

Source	D	Seq SS	Adj SS	Adj MS	F	P
Main Effects	5	1205.7	1205.7	241.14	2.93	0.111
2-Way Interactions	10	422.9	422.9	42.29	0.51	0.832
3-Way Interactions	10	624.0	624.0	62.40	0.76	0.667
Residual Error	6	493.5	493.5	82.26		
Total	31	2746.1				

The above results show the impact the chosen variables had on the overall observed variation.

ε^2 = Sum of all Seq. SS less error / Seq. SS Total = 2252.6 / 2746.1 = **82 %**

This means that 82% of the observed variation can be controlled by the 5 factors chosen in the experiment.

Intro | Ready ? | 6 Months | Project | Long Haul | DMAIIC | Tools | R & R

Machado could sense they were losing the team's attention. At the next pause in the presentation, he suggested to Carlos that they cover the Main Effects Plot and the Pareto first and come back to the numbers later.

"Thanks, Gil, but I think we all need to learn how to deal with the data we worked so hard to collect."

Aguiar wasn't happy with Machado's interruption or the way he babied the team. He continued on and didn't get to the Main Effects and Pareto charts until after lunch.

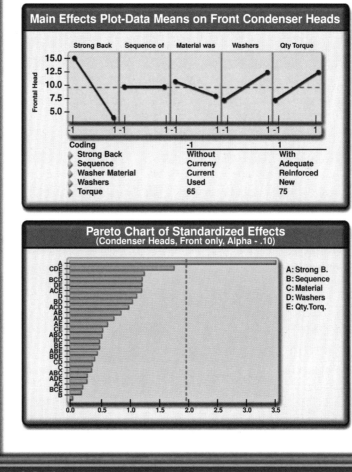

© *2001 Brassard & Ritter, LLC*

When Carlos finally did display the Main Effects and Pareto diagrams side by side, he realized he should have listened to Gil Machado's suggestion earlier in the meeting. The once quiet meeting took on new life.

> *"I didn't think the torque sequence would matter, but I was surprised that the heavier washers didn't make a bigger difference. We'd all guessed Strong Back would be the key, but Antonio asked if we could take another look at the details about it in combination with other factors. I'm glad we went back to review it."*

First Shift Manager,
TL member (through interpreter)

Questions started flying… people were interrupting each other… the whole team was involved. Carlos looked over at Gil, shrugged his shoulders and smiled. He knew that by Monday's meeting Team Leaks would be ready to start planning for countermeasures—just the news Camden was waiting to hear. Maybe now they'd get off his back.

Week 19 — September 6, 1999
The room was buzzing. The members of the team were huddled in two's and three's around the conference table. Since last week's meeting—just as Carlos Aguiar and Gil Machado had asked—each of them had been thinking about ways to implement the process and material changes they'd identified in their Design of Experiments. Today was the day they'd move from planning, to doing, to fixing the condenser-leak problem for good.

They quieted down as team leader Aguiar ceremoniously hung a single sheet of flip-chart paper on the wall. On it was an empty matrix diagram with the simple, one-word heading– "Countermeasures." By meeting's end, the matrix was complete and each of them was prepared to lead or support a sub-team focused on a

Intro

Ready ?

6 Months

Project

Long Haul

DMAIIC

Tools

R & R

single countermeasure. By mid-to-late October, they would start seeing results. They were psyched.

Countermeasures

	WHAT	WHO	WHEN	STATUS
	(Action)	(Responsibility)	(Start)	(Finish)
1	Strong Back implementation	Team Leaks	13-Sep-99	20-Sep-99
2	Torque procedure standardization	S. Aguiar	13-Sep-99	20-Sep-99
3	Heavier Duty Washers (purchasing)	L. Campos	13 Sep-99	Ongoing
4	Akron Plant site visit	J. Cabral	13-Dec-99	17-Dec-99

Week 33 — December 17, 1999

At the September 22nd team meeting, Carlos Aguiar had announced that Team Leaks would no longer meet every week. Instead, the bi-weekly review meetings would be extended from 30 to 90 minutes and cover some of the day-to-day issues along with project and data updates.

Though it had been too early to tell if the gains were real, the review meetings in October, November and early December had been the most positive sessions of the project. With the exception of a claims spike (9) the last full week of November, the numbers of leaks had been significantly—but not yet satisfactorily—reduced.

The "Special Cause" sub-team's report to the group shed some light on the November spike. They pointed out that, during that week, four out of sixteen line managers (three from the first shift and one from the second) had noted on their QA reports, "recalibrated Strong Back after distortion tolerances were exceeded" or something very similar.

Everyone agreed with the sub-team's recommendation that they meet with production inspectors from both the first and second shifts, to plan an immediate Strong Back calibration check on all lines. They promised a follow-up report at the next meeting.

Week 35 — December 31, 1999

Because it was New Year's Eve, the team had agreed to hold its bi-weekly review in the morning instead of late afternoon. The last meeting of 1999 ended up being a turning point for Team Leaks. It resulted in two more changes to the Santos manufacturing process—changes that were minor, yet critical to the achievement of the team's Six Sigma goals.

First up was the Speical Cause sub-team's follow-up report on the Strong Back calibration problem. In their research, they had discovered a serious situation—all Strong Back units in the plant needed recalibration, even the four that had been previously adjusted. Although their actions had been too late to prevent another even more significant spike in leak claims (15) the week of December 13th, the numbers following their recalibrations had returned to the new, lower "normal" levels.

The sub-team suggested scheduling a Strong Back recalibration on each line at the end of each shift—a five-minute operation. The team approved the recommendation and assigned the production inspectors the immediate task of training the line managers on their respective shifts in the simple new procedure. The daily recalibrations were to begin the second week of January.

The next item on the agenda was QA Manager's Jorge Cabral's report on his site visit to the Akron plant earlier in the month. Cabral explained to the team how it had been a rather uneventful week until the day before he was scheduled to fly home. Then, while having lunch with a couple of field techs from California, he'd simply asked them how *they* fixed condenser leaks on the job.

"That's when they showed me these special little washer gaskets they'd rigged up. They said that they worked every time and seemed to last forever."

Cabral reached into his pocket and plunked a handful of the hand-cut gaskets onto the conference table. After a quick inspection of the gaskets, the team's production engineer estimated they would cost no more than 10¢ each to make, or less than $5.00 per condenser. The presentation ended with a question:

"Wouldn't a simple, inexpensive back-end fix such as this make more sense on the front end... our end?"

The group agreed.

Intro

Ready ?

6 Months

Project

Long Haul

DMAIIC

Tools

R & R

Intro

Ready ?

6 Months

Project

Long Haul

DMAIIC

Tools

R & R

> "This team
> was really starting to manage
> itself. When they saw a problem, they
> fixed it, and I wasn't about to stand in their way.
> So, I asked them to work up design specs by Monday
> afternoon. I called purchasing right from the
> meeting room. I wanted those gaskets
> on line by January 12th."

Carlos Aguiar
Plant Manager, Team Leaks Project Leader

May 31, 2000
Three months after the official end of the project...

The members of Team Leaks milled around, talking, drinking sodas, and munching on snacks from a table in the far corner of the conference room. Other than the snack table, there were no other furnishings except the three festively wrapped flip chart easels sitting in the center of the room.

After twenty minutes or so, Carlos Aguiar gathered the team around the easels. He began to speak, dramatically unwrapping the flip charts as he referred to them:

"I think you guys might suspect why we're here. Although I've thanked each of you individually, I just thought the project team might want to meet one more time to celebrate your huge success with Alphamega's first Six Sigma effort. Just look at the most recent numbers Team Leaks is responsible for..."

"In the 27 weeks before all corrective actions went into effect, we received 240 head leak claims—almost 10 per week. In Six Sigma terms, we were running at a 3.4 Sigma level. If we hadn't made the improvements to the process we would produce nearly 23,000 defects per million opportunities! Remember that we refer to that as "DPMO"? How do you think our customers would feel about that number? Since your corrective actions? 15 claims in 17 weeks—that's less than 1 claim per week! We improved to a 4.4

Intro

Ready ?

6 Months

Project

Long Haul

DMAIIC

Tools

R & R

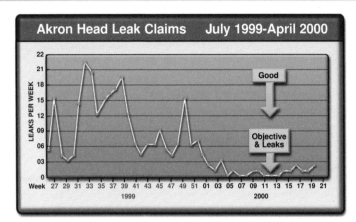

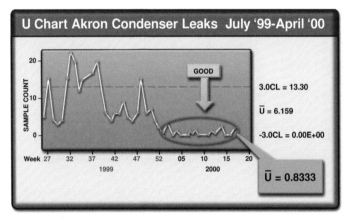

Sigma level. This means that as long as we hold onto this improvement we'll deliver only about 1600 DPMO! At that rate we'll be spending around $50K in condenser leak warranty repairs as opposed to $580K last year. That's $540K that goes straight to our bottom-line.

It's an incredible change, but I also want to ask you to keep thinking about ways to make the process even better. Think about this... .If we ever were able to get our production process to a Six Sigma level we would produce only 3.4 Defects per Million Opportunities! At that level, Akron wouldn't even have to inspect

Intro

Ready ?

6 Months

Project

Long Haul

DMAIIC

Tools

R & R

our condensers. They'd just install the units with absolute confidence in them, AND in us.

Let's finish up by taking a look at the next steps for our group that we discussed at our final project meeting on March 3rd. I listed them on the flip chart and I've made copies for you to take on the way out. Thanks again, guys, for a job well done."

Team Leaks - Next Steps

1.) Remain as a team primarily for communications and advisory purposes (on call), and for quarterly condenser leak "check ins."

2.) Continue to support Jorge Cabral, the QA Manager and Gil Machado, the Black Belt, as they gather head-leak data and analyze it using Pareto, Run, and Control Charts over the next year.

3.) Continue to deliver and support operator training in new processes.

4.) Follow up on standard operating procedures for torque control.

5.) Monitor for retorque/torque loss at Akron.

"Oh, and one last thing, the people in Camden asked me to give you a round of applause from them and tell you 'the check is in the mail'—bonuses will be paid on January 15, 2001 for total savings on condenser leak claims for the whole calendar year 2000 vs. 1999. You guys deserve it after all your hard work... even when I made your lives miserable!"

Laughing, the group filed out of the conference room. Carlos turned off the light and closed the door behind him.

Let's review the process and results of the ARC case study using the DMAIIC framework:

Intro

Ready ?

6 Months

Project

Long Haul

DMAIIC

Tools

R & R

ARC Project Overview

Define
- ✓ "Qualified" the Condenser Leak project due to its connection to Warranty Costs, a KPI, and the sizeable $580K improvement target.
- ✓ Chartered and launched the project team, "Team Leaks", which represented a cross-section of the Santos plant's operation.

Measure
- ✓ Reviewed historical data and collected two weeks of process data to measure current process performance.
- ✓ Refined the problem statement to "Condenser Head Leaks."

Analyze
- ✓ Completed a Cause & Effect analysis based upon the historical data, the two-week intense observation of the process and the personal experience and knowledge of the team members.
- ✓ Conducted a five factor, two-level Designed Experiment to identify the root cause from among the causal factors identified by the team.
- ✓ Identified three leading causal factors: Strong Back, Torque Sequence, and Washer Material (in descending order of influence).

Improve
- ✓ Developed countermeasures and an action plan (*What*, *Who*, and *When*) to eliminate/reduce the root causes.

Implement
- ✓ Instituted the process, procedural and materials changes.
- ✓ Measured performance over a three-month period.
- ✓ Uncovered deeper process problems (Strong Back Calibration) and another materials-based solution (a redesigned, inexpensive gasket already in use at another ARC plant).
- ✓ Amended the countermeasures and created a revised action plan. *Continued on next page...*

Intro
Ready ?
6 Months
Project
Long Haul
DMAIIC
Tools
R & R

ARC Project Overview *(continued)*

Control
✓ Assigned the QA Manager and Black Belt to continue to collect and analyze "Head Leak" data with the authority to reconvene the team as needed.

✓ Created training to support the new Standard Operating Procedures.

✓ Established ongoing relationships with internal customers at US plants to monitor the impact of the changed processes.

Results

Quantifiable...
✓ Improved process performance from 3.4 to 4.4 Sigma (from 22,910 DPMO to 1629 DPMO).

✓ Saved $540K in warranty repair costs.

✓ Reduced the rate of condenser leak warranty claims from 10/week to less than 1/week.

Qualitative...
✓ Issues of language and culture that plagued the relationship between the Brazilian and American operations were dramatically improved. By using the language of data, 6σ as the standard for excellence, and the culture of never-ending Six Sigma improvement, an organizational bridge was built that can now be used for tackling even tougher issues.

✓ A project team of line managers (and one Plant Manager) was trained in the philosophy, process and tools of Six Sigma.

✓ The Santos plant was now seen as a more reliable, responsive supplier. It's much more likely that corporate leaders would look to the plant to produce new, critical components for products under development.

Expert Advice:

Lesson #1 – *Confirm before proceeding that bottom line results are significant and worth pursuing.*

Confirm Savings – Before making any project selection, get the Chief Financial Officer (CFO) or the equivalent-level manager in your business unit, to confirm the projected savings. Everyone in the organization has to trust the numbers from the beginning...no "funny money."

Think Big – If your improvement targets represent less than a 50% reduction or 100% increase in the critical measure, review your assumptions or look elsewhere for more significant opportunities.

Think Pareto – Choose projects from your top 5 Cost of Poor Quality (COPQ) categories. Anything lower in the Pareto may be "important, but not life-threatening."

Think Revenue Too – Work both sides of the P & L. Projects that *make* money (revenue-generators) are just as valuable as those that *save* money (cost-cutters).

Work To The Limit Of Your Resources – Continue to generate projects until you run out of resources to support them. In other words, keep attacking bars on the Pareto Chart with projects until all resources are exhausted.

In ARC's Case...

The Condenser Leak problem passed the "tallest-bar-on-the-Pareto" test, but was it the most critical defect to the customer? Was the Condenser Leak a serious, but not catastrophic, failure for the customer? Would a less costly rework item (for ARC) like "Motor Failure" have a greater impact on future customer purchases than Condenser Leaks? This last question should have been answered in order to stay focused on the most important selection criteria: "*Overall* Impact on the Business Bottom Line."

Intro

Ready ?

6 Months

Project

Long Haul

DMAIIC

Tools

R & R

Lesson #2 – *Set up an implementation & progress review schedule that creates and maintains a sense of urgency*

The Optimum Project Schedule – Black Belt Six Sigma projects take an average of four to eight months to complete. However, six months seems to be the ideal project time frame – long enough to undertake major process changes, but short enough to stay within an organization's "attention-span." If it's projected to exceed the six-month timeframe, consider splitting the project into two or more parts. Having said this, there are leading Six Sigma companies that are considerably more aggressive, using *3 months* as the target completion time. Once again, fit your culture, BUT choose a target time that's significantly faster than your historical norm.

In Case Of An Emergency – On average, project teams meet once every one to two weeks, with reviews scheduled monthly. However, would this be an appropriate schedule if a problem represented a $250K monthly loss, as compared to the $50K monthly loss, in the ARC case study? Probably not. Here's an emergency strategy:

1. Estimate the *workload* (e.g. entire dedicated project time=160 hours) for the team.

2. Estimate the *shortest time period* in which the *workload* could *possibly* be accomplished (e.g. 6 weeks). Allow for necessary elapsed time for things such as process experimentation, but assume that the team has no other responsibilities.

3. Calculate the *loss avoidance* of resolving the problem with a full-time team (or as close as possible), rather than a part-time team.

4. Create a "hyper-speed" review schedule based on mile stones, NOT the calendar. Conduct reviews when:

   a. The problem statement has been created.

   b. The root causes have been validated.

   c. The action plan has been drafted.

   d. The pilot implementation is completed and the control plan is in place.

Intro

Ready ?

6 Months

Project

Long Haul

DMAIIC

Tools

R & R

In ARC's Case...

The DOE process appeared to be held up by conflicting production requirements and some missed assignments. Neither of these
are unusual situations, but the Plant Manager, the project leader,
had both of these factors under his control. Even savinga month
from the schedule would have in-creased the potential project
savings by almost $50K! Once a loss has been incurred, it's
gone forever.

**Lesson #3 – Meet the needs of ALL of the players on the team
so that they can fully contribute to the success of the project.**

Project Team Members – One of the most valuable roles of the
Black Belt is to assess the needs of each project team and either
provide or arrange for the training (in both "soft" and "hard" skills)
to be delivered "just-in-time." A foolproof method of "invisible"
training is to provide a constant flow of examples and applications
of Six Sigma from other departments or companies. This builds
both motivation and application knowledge.

Process Owner/ Manager – The Black Belt must devote individual
attention to the process owner (even when the Black Belt is the
project leader) to assess his or her knowledge and skills in playing a
leadership role in the Six Sigma team. Green Belt training should
supply the basics, but the Black Belt must confirm that the training
"took" and be prepared to fill any knowledge gaps that appear. It's
the Black Belt's job to ensure that the manager has enough *competence* and *confidence* to be viewed by the team as a full project partner, and NOT as a slave to the Black Belt.

Black Belts – Black Belts are such vital resources that *their* needs
are often overlooked in the process. Day-to-day Black Belt support
comes primarily from Master Black Belts, Project Champions and
other Black Belts.

- *Master Black Belts* (or the external consultants in first-
  round programs) must be "on call" for mentoring and technical questions. They must also be available for formal,
  mid- and post-project reviews.

> *Black
> Belts become
> **mentors**.
> not masters
> to process
> owners/
> managers*

Intro

Ready ?

6 Months

Project

Long Haul

DMAIIC

Tools

R & R

NEVER let an under-performing Black Belt flounder. You risk an invaluable resource AND the credibility of Six Sigma

- *Champions* must go to bat for Black Belts in the inevitable turf battles over authority and resources that happen during the course of a project.

- *Black Belts can* support each other in a number of practical ways: monthly best practice workshops; lunches; Intranet chat rooms; joint skills training; daily "can-I-bounce-an-idea-off-you" telephone calls.

In ARC's Case...

Gil Machado, the Black Belt did a nice job recognizing when the team needed training in DOE, Project Management and Team Skills. He also showed support and deference to Carlos Aguiar, the Plant Manager/Project Leader. In fact, at times he was a bit too deferential. He could have been more aggressive on the issues of the project schedule and meeting agend as since he was the Six Sigma process expert and mentor. If the Plant Manager ignored his advice, Gil could have turned to others, like the Project Champion, to help influence the situation.

Warning #1 – *Don't allow managers and teams to opt out of the review process.*

There is nothing more important to a successful DMAIIC project than regularly scheduled, consistent and positive *Progress Reviews*. The standard review checklist and meeting agenda described in the project template above provides a great foundation. However, **100% participation** by the managers and team members is even more fundamental. The beginning of the end comes when *anyone* is allowed to miss review meetings. This is an extreme, but necessary standard of behavior. How can a team live up to such a standard?

1. Black Belts must train and support managers in conducting reviews – train them, demonstrate the process, observe them in reviews, coach them for the life of the project.

2. Schedule all of the standard reviews at the *beginning* of the project.

3. Schedule the project review meetings on the same day as "sacred" meetings, such as operations reviews.

4. Document attendance (and absent members) within the minutes of the meeting and distribute them to the Lead Team and Champions.

5. Ensure that reviews are scheduled to match the pace of the project.

6. Create tight agendas that are distributed at least several days before the meeting.

In ARC's Case...

"Team Leaks" is a classic example of the "slippery slope" that begins when the Process Owner/Manager excuses him/herself from a progress review. It gives other members of the team the green light to do the same. This is another instance when the team's Black Belt (in his mentor role) could have been more assertive with the Plant Manager. Instead, the Black Belt worked harder. If he hadn't been there to keep the team on track, it could easily have floundered. It worked out in the end, BUT did the team members (especially the Plant Manager) actually *learn* how to use reviews to stay on track for the *next* project team they're on?

Warning #2 – *Don't hinder Black Belts from doing their work.*

Eliminate unnecessary administrative load – Black Belts could easily spend their time updating the organization on project status. Instead, create a single "DMAIIC Story" (GE uses a form called the "4-UP" for this purpose) that communicates the history, action plan and status of the project. Create an "open-book" approach to communication by making the DMAIIC Story and supporting data available to everyone in the organization. This can be posted either on a company Intranet, Six Sigma bulletin board/information center, or in a "Project Binder" that's available in a central location.

Intro

Ready ?

6 Months

Project

Long Haul

DMAIIC

Tools

R & R

Intro

Ready ?

6 Months

Project

Long Haul

DMAIIC

Tools

R & R

Don't create teams with built-in "failure-modes."

Some team failure modes that can be anticipated and avoided:

✓ *Rotating different people through a team based on the assumption that people are interchangeable.* Ad hoc membership is fine for specialists who "join" the team, give their input and leave. Rotating core team members wreaks havoc on the continuity and productivity of the team.

✓ *Withholding talented people who are "too valuable" to be dedicated to a Six Sigma team.* If this happens, look closely at the topic that a team is undertaking. If the project doesn't deserve the talents of the "best and the brightest," perhaps it's a poor choice. Six Sigma targets should be so close to the core of the business that you would commit *only* your best people to the project.

✓ *Failing to give team members what they need to fully con tribute to the team.* Below is a commitment checklist for managers of potential project team members:

• Will you commit some of your key personnel to 2 to 20 hours per week for up to 6 months?

• Will you make it possible for them to attend an average of 2-3 days of skills training?

• Will you support the team members in meeting team commitments even when those commitments conflict with ongoing operations?

• Are you willing to be held accountable for your level of support (or lack thereof) for the work of the team?

 Spillover Advice...

In this section, the key Lessons and Warnings from Six Sigma experts are included in the book. Other important Lessons and Warnings are listed below. Once in the e-book, just click on the Idea icon next to the Lessons or Warnings # you want to view in its entirety.

Warning #3 – *Don't become a slave to the tools.*

Warning #4 – *Don't treat teams differently than you would treat individuals.*

Warning #5 – *Don't overload people with unnecessary training...but give them what they need.*

 ## The Check List:

Have you...

- ☐ Completed the DMAIIC model steps?

- ☐ Assessed your progress in 6σ measurement terms?

- ☐ Improved the selected Key Performance Indicator (KPI) by the targeted amount?

- ☐ Established a solid control plan to monitor and hold the gains that were achieved in the project?

- ☐ Developed the improvement skills of the project team members and Six Sigma "players"?

- ☐ Celebrated and recognized the hard work and achievements of both the direct and indirect contributors to the success of the project?

Intro

Ready ?

6 Months

Project

Long Haul

DMAIIC

Tools

R & R

Intro

Ready ?

6 Months

Project

Long Haul

DMAIIC

Tools

R & R

Chapter 5:
The Long Haul

Taking Six Sigma from a program with a definable life-span to a way-of-life management system

Purpose of this chapter:

To describe what leaders at all levels must do to ensure that "over the long haul" people *naturally* measure, manage and improve their processes using the Six Sigma philosophy and methods.

For senior executives this chapter...

- Previews the next round of improvement targets after successfully completing the Six Sigma pilot phase.
- Describes the deeper system changes that will have to be made to move Six Sigma from an improvement program to a management process.

For managers at all levels this chapter...

- Provides a glimpse of your future role as a process owner/manager.
- Describes the process for designing new processes with Six Sigma capabilities built in, rather than "simply" improving existing ones.
- Provides simple, but powerful, ways to make "Six Sigma process thinking" a part of your daily management style.

The Big Picture:

Year 1: Planning & Building a Six Sigma Track record

The first year of a Six Sigma program is designed to accomplish two things:

- To build the *credibility* of the Six Sigma process by creating a significant impact on the bottom-line of the business.

Intro

Ready ?

6 Months

Project

Long Haul

DMAIIC

Tools

R & R

Intro
Ready ?
6 Months
Project
Long Haul
DMAIIC
Tools
R & R

- To ensure that EVERY player (Champions, Black Belts, Green Belts and Team Members) has *competence* and *confidence* in Six Sigma as a mindset, methodology and measure.

As in any major change process, however, there is one nagging question after the first year of implementing Six Sigma:

How can we keep up this pace and intensity?

The rest of the chapter provides proven strategies to meet this challenge.

Year 2: Expanding the application of Six Sigma

If the first year is about building a track record, then the second year is about aiming the Six Sigma process at an ever-expanding set of improvement targets. The goal is to "surround people with change," so that anyone who is not fully participating in Six Sigma feels out of step with the strategic future of the organization. There are three ways to accomplish this "*positive pressure to change*":

1. **Leverage Existing Six Sigma Resources**
   → Chase Bigger Targets → Create Higher Visibility → **Positive Pressure to be Recognized**

2. **Expand Six Sigma Resources**
   → Widen the Variety of Applications → Create a More Pervasive Presence → **Positive Pressure to fully Participative**

3. **Change Current Management Systems**
   → Prove that It's NOT "Business-as-Usual" → Show Serious Intent → **Positive Pressure to Align with the Strategic Direction.**

Intro

Ready ?

6 Months

Project

Long Haul

DMAIIC

Tools

R & R

1. **Leverage Existing Six Sigma Resources – Create new challenges for your first-round Black Belts and Green Belts.**

   Pushing those trained as Black Belts to tackle more challenging assignments has obvious benefits to the organization: an enormous increase both in the return on the training investment and on the financial impact of Six Sigma.

   The increased challenge is also critical for the Black Belts themselves. Think about it. You've plucked some of the most talented, motivated individuals from the day-to-day operations. By definition, they're "hungry" for new skills and ways to test those skills. They're looking for an "Improvement MBA" that they can take back with them after their 2-year assignment (the recommended time period).

   To create this challenge for Black Belts and Green Belts:
   - Certified Black Belts should tackle DMAIIC projects that cut across processes, facilities and divisions. In projects that may involve improving company-wide systems, they can team with either a Master Black Belt or another Black Belt.
   - Second-year Green Belts must also take on increasingly more complex, higher impact projects in their own processes or departments.
   - Require that all of the certified "Belts" be even more productive in the second year because of their deeper experience in both Project Management and the DMAIIC process itself.

     Black Belts – 3-4 typical projects (some companies claim 5-6 projects/year).
     Green Belts – 2 significant projects/year plus "mini-projects" (completed in weeks vs. months)
   - Black Belts should move beyond improving existing processes and products (using DMAIIC) to creating new processes and products (using Design for Six Sigma – DFSS) that have 6σ performance built into them. In some implementation models Black Belts must go through an additional 3-4 weeks of DFSS training before starting a

Intro

Ready ?

6 Months

Project

Long Haul

DMAIIC

Tools

R & R

DFSS project. Other models include such DFSS training as part of the first-round curriculum. This second approach assumes that the Master Black Belt will "shadow" Black Belts assigned for the first time to DFSS projects.

2. Expand Six Sigma Resources – Dramatically increase the number of Black Belts and Green Belts, allowing Six Sigma to expand into non-manufacturing operations.

Consider the following statistics taken from the article, "Expanding Six Sigma," by Bill Schmitt in the February 22, 2001 issue of Chemical Week:

- Since launching Six Sigma two years ago, DuPont has trained 160 Master Black Belts and over 1100 Black Belts (just over 1% of its 90K+ employees) who have worked on about 3500 projects. 2100 Green Belts have been added over the last year alone. DuPont is currently achieving roughly $1 billion in annual savings or revenue. Savings initially came from the manufacturing sector, but now a third of projects are in corporate services such as sales, finance and human resources.

- W.R. Grace will add 12 more Black Belts during 2001. This will bring the total up to their target of 60 (1% of its 6000 person workforce). The company is now focusing more on training Green Belts in order to "make Six Sigma more a way of life." Grace expects to generate over $40 million in financial benefits in addition to the $33 million achieved in 2000.

These companies seem to be heeding the lessons learned by General Electric in the mid 90's. GE realized after the first year of incredibly intense training and impressive results, that there would never be enough Black Belts to move the entire corporation to Six Sigma performance. The key was to train and support (a key role for Black Belts) thousands of part-time Green Belts, drawn from the ranks of managers and professionals.

Intro

Ready ?

6 Months

Project

Long Haul

DMAIIC

Tools

R & R

> **The lesson for Year 2:**
> Continue building the cadre of Black Belts toward the ideal 1%-of-total-employees level while producing *as many Green Belts as the Six Sigma infrastructure can support.*

3. Begin changing management systems that support Six Sigma.

Now (in the second year of implementation) is the time to *refine/redesign* systems so that they can reinforce Six Sigma values and processes as permanent parts of the organizational fabric.

Reward & Recognition: At a minimum, Six Sigma project support and skills shown by managers should now be included in individual performance reviews:

- For the current Green Belts set the expectations at the beginning of the year that they must complete at least two significant projects. For non-Green Belts at the start of the year require that they identify the project that they will complete as part of their training. Assess all Green Belts ("veterans" and "rookies") on the impact of their project(s) and their personal contribution to the project in their year-end performance review.

- If your organization has a management bonus system, you can follow the "GE Model" in Year Two: no significant Six Sigma project – no bonus. In order to prevent this from becoming a "just-get-any-project-done" approach, the project must have a *direct and meaningful impact* on a manager's Key Performance Indicators (KPI's).

These are both powerful signs of leadership commitment, but the greatest *long-term* impact comes from changing the criteria for promotions. At GE it's now assumed that all "early-career top 20% performers" will take on a 2-3 year Black Belt assignment to prepare them for their future leadership roles. This clearly maps the strategic course of the "corporate ship" AND who will be "at its wheel" in the not-too-distant future.

Operations Reviews: During regular monthly reviews of business operations, include status reports of both the *process* and the *results* of Six Sigma by:

- Starting with the KPI's and evaluating projects (and ALL other reviewed activities) based upon their impact on these performance measures.

- Adjusting both the pace and focus of projects (as well as initiating or abandoning projects) based on their impact on key measures.

Budgeting: Synchronize the setting of the year's Six Sigma targets, training plan, and projects and supporting budgets with the strategic planning and budgeting process.

> To reinforce the critical importance of Six Sigma projects, develop budgets that assume that the projected Six Sigma savings WILL indeed occur. This "hardwired budget" guarantees that everyone will choose their improvement targets *carefully* and pursue them *seriously*.

Year 3: Improving the application of Six Sigma

The third year of implementation is the year in which an organization must "take ownership" for its long-term Six Sigma model by:

- *Improving* the model.
- *Invigorating* the process.
- *Internalizing* the resources.

Improving the model

By this point an organization will have completed a significant number of projects in a wide variety of applications. This experience base reveals the strengths and weaknesses of the Six Sigma model (the improvement steps, training protocol, staffing, etc.) as it was originally implemented.

Any weakness that makes projects *less efficient* (slower results and increased investment) and less *predictable* (more variation and lower return) must be addressed to ensure Six Sigma's business credibility. Some problem areas that typically surface at this stage:

- **Project selection:** Encouraging non-traditional applications; setting more dramatic targets.
- **Team selection:** Preventing "burn-out"; keeping project teams as lean as possible.
- **Black Belt selection:** Going broader and deeper into the organization to identify Black Belt candidates; supporting Black Belts who are struggling.
- **Training design and delivery**: Keeping pace with attrition and turnover rates; reducing variation in student performance across instructors.
- **Team performance:** Varying attendance at team meetings as Six Sigma becomes "old hat"; missing projected deadlines.
- **Reviews:** Delaying project reviews because they conflict with "real business"; designing more efficient review sessions.

Invigorating the process

Involve the supply chain in Six Sigma: Based on the principle of "surrounding people with change," there's a constant need for the Six Sigma process to touch new people, new departments, new functions. For the first two years this contagion effect happens internally. By the third year a Six Sigma organization is finally ready to "infect" the most leveraged part of the system: its supply chain.

It's logical (and typical) to first target your most critical suppliers since Six Sigma performance in their processes immediately improves your cost structure. Choose carefully, since Six Sigma is such a major commitment for both parties.

- For example, as of mid-1998, 150 suppliers to GE's Aircraft Engine Division (GE started its implementation

Intro

Ready ?

6 Months

Project

Long Haul

DMAIC

Tools

R & R

in 1995) had employees trained as Black Belts, but only 16 of those companies had committed to a full-scale implementation.

It's also time to work with the other end of the supply chain: key customers. The article, "GE Takes Six Sigma Beyond The Bottom Line," by Gregory Lucier and Sridhar Seshadri in the May 2001 issue of *Strategic Finance,* includes some GE supply-chain results involving customers.

- In GE Medical Systems alone there were over 1100 Six Sigma projects involving customers by the end of 2000. 466 customer projects completed in last year alone saved over $91 million.

- GE helped Commonwealth Health Corporation of Kentucky apply Six Sigma, resulting in over $1.5 million in savings and a dramatically different company culture.

Whether you make the business decision to assist critical suppliers or key customers, this involvement of the "outside world" in Six Sigma sets off a chain reaction that solidifies internal support for the process.

Supply-Chain Reaction

If you're a Six Sigma company that's....

Enabling customers to improve their bottom-line, it normally leads to a growing business relationship.

Enabling suppliers to generate savings, it improves the cost structure of their products.

Improved profitability for the Six Sigma "enabling company"

An improved bottom-line that reinforces the business benefits of (and managerial enthusiasm for) Six Sigma.

Intro
Ready ?
6 Months
Project
Long Haul
DMAIIC
Tools
R & R

Tackle lingering (and long-term) change management issues:
A long, honest look in the mirror is one of the most effective and energizing ways for an organization to "own" the Six Sigma process as it has evolved over the first two years of implementation. Everyone who has led or participated in teams should be involved in diagnosing problem-areas and suggesting program changes. Design the self-exam in a way that fits your culture:

- Business-unit meetings
- Intranet-discussion groups
- Open-invitation improvement "summits"
- Written surveys

In any study format, be sure to answer these questions that are critical to implementing major cultural changes:

1. Is the program of a manageable size?
2. Does it have clear and unchanging focus?
3. Does it focus first, and foremost, on results?
4. Are the measurements used truly tied to the success of the business?
5. Is the process driven by "line" leadership, rather than by staff functions or consultants?
6. Is it more important to "do it by the book" than to use data to show what's really producing results?

Internalizing the resources.

External consultants play a number of vital roles in introducing Six Sigma into a company. However, by the third year, program leadership and expertise MUST be transferred to internal players. The only proven, planned way to make this happen is to build up two critical roles:

- *The Deployment/Program Champion* – The Program Champion is the CEO's surrogate for the day-to-day management of Six Sigma implementation. The ideal Champion MUST therefore have the credibility and presence to speak and act for the CEO, as would a

Intro

Ready ?

6 Months

Project

Long Haul

DMAIC

Tools

R & R

Chief Operating Officer (COO). Also, like a COO, a Champion must combine *high energy and deep experience in the core business* in order to be effective.

- *The Master Black Belts* – As the technical Six Sigma experts, Master Black Belts must direct, design and deliver when needed all team and "belt" training, including certification programs. This workload dictates that there be *one* Master Black Belt for every *fifteen to twenty* Black Belts. This is not a place to cut corners!

 Expert Advice:

Lesson #1 – *Integrate Six Sigma into a broader system of Process-Focused Management.*

Six Sigma can be treated as a tool to dramatically improve "broken processes" and to create processes from scratch that produce nearly perfect products and services. This "tool-in-our-improvement-toolkit" approach can have a tremendous impact on the bottom-line *over the first 18-24 months of implementation*. However, Six Sigma will become a *permanent* fixture only when it flows naturally from a "process-focused management" system.

Five Steps to Practicing Process-Focused Management.

#1. View the organization as a system of interdependent processes rather than as independent functions within a hierarchy.

A Hierarchical View Is…	A Hierarchical View Isn't…
…neat.	…helpful in describing how customers are served.
…easy to draw.	
…a great way to capture reporting relationships.	…helpful in showing how information flows (or needs to flow).
…convenient for communicating functional or department goals.	…reflective of how work actually happens.

It's not that viewing an organization as a hierarchy is "bad;" it's just not very helpful in defining what's important to measure and improve to better serve the customer.

Intro

Ready ?

6 Months

Project

Long Haul

DMAIIC

Tools

R & R

Intro

Ready ?

6 Months

Project

Long Haul

DMAIC

Tools

R & R

Dr. Deming drew the prototype of a "systems view" of an organization during his now-famous lectures in Japan in 1950.

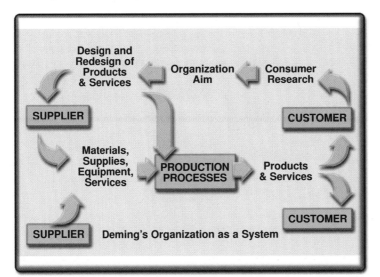

Deming's Organization as a System

The beauty of this view is that every link between processes automatically reveals a *customer-supplier relationship* that must be constantly managed. This model applies to *every* organization of *any* size in *all* industries. Simply include the basic steps in your "production process" and it is now a picture of *your* system.

#2. Link and align the aims/strategies of the business to all of the critical processes.

At the simplest level, the operation of any organization can be reduced to a tree diagram with processes (cutting across functions) that *should* all fully contribute to successfully achieving the company strategy. This is called "alignment."

Alignment means that everyone involved in the processes *knows* what they need to do to support the next-highest process, and ultimately the company strategy… and then *performs* to that expectation.

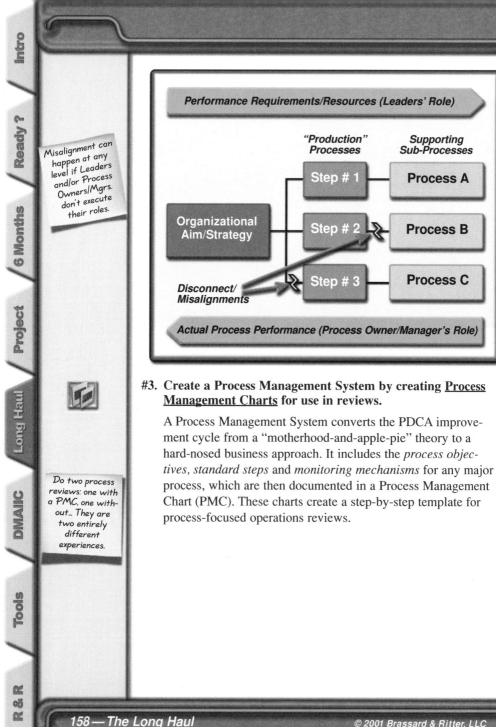

Intro

Ready ?

6 Months

Project

Long Haul

DMAIIC

Tools

R & R

Misalignment can happen at any level if Leaders and/or Process Owners/Mgrs. don't execute their roles.

Do two process reviews: one with a PMC, one without... They are two entirely different experiences.

#3. **Create a Process Management System by creating <u>Process Management Charts</u> for use in reviews.**

A Process Management System converts the PDCA improvement cycle from a "motherhood-and-apple-pie" theory to a hard-nosed business approach. It includes the *process objectives, standard steps* and *monitoring mechanisms* for any major process, which are then documented in a Process Management Chart (PMC). These charts create a step-by-step template for process-focused operations reviews.

#4. Create, manage and improve the processes.

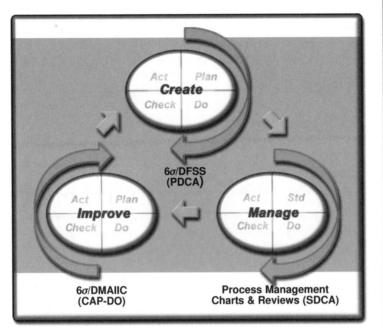

#5. Align Daily Management Behavior.

The final, and most critical, step is aligning your own personal behavior and approach with maintaining and improving performance with Six Sigma. Only this level of personal commitment will convince people that you lead, that the formal Six Sigma process is simply the way that work gets done. It's your job to communicate and reinforce this by:

- Asking guiding questions that encourage your reports to "think process."
- Making (and asking for) data-based decisions.
- Fixing *processes* rather than *blame* for performance problems.
- Documenting key processes and reviewing their performance *at least* monthly.

Intro

Ready ?

6 Months

Project

Long Haul

DMAIIC

Tools

R & R

Lesson #2 – *Get some Design For Six Sigma (DFSS) successes.*

DMAIIC, with its cost-savings impact, is the primary focus for the early stages of Six Sigma implementation. It can be (and is) used to generate new revenue, but this outcome is the real strength of the DFSS process. It's critical to stress this "growing-the-business" dimension of Six Sigma since revenue growth is at the heart of every business model. If Six Sigma is seen as an ongoing growth "engine," managers at all levels will view it as part of the permanent management system, not as an initiative that can be ignored.

The Basics of DFSS

At its absolute simplest DFSS focuses on:

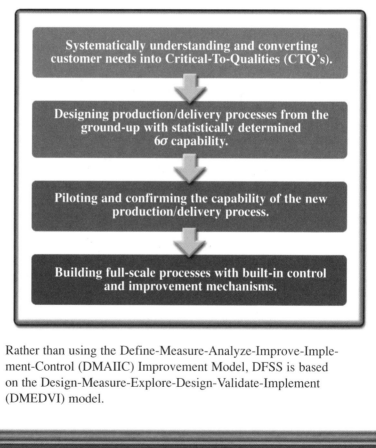

Systematically understanding and converting customer needs into Critical-To-Qualities (CTQ's).

Designing production/delivery processes from the ground-up with statistically determined 6σ capability.

Piloting and confirming the capability of the new production/delivery process.

Building full-scale processes with built-in control and improvement mechanisms.

Rather than using the Define-Measure-Analyze-Improve-Implement-Control (DMAIIC) Improvement Model, DFSS is based on the Design-Measure-Explore-Design-Validate-Implement (DMEDVI) model.

Intro

Ready ?

6 Months

Project

Long Haul

DMAIIC

Tools

R & R

DMEDVI*	Steps
Define	1. Launch the Project 2. Define Outcomes 3. Identify Stakeholders 4. Select Team 5. Determine Project Approach 6. Create Project Plan
Measure	1. Identify Customers 2. Define State of Current customer Knowledge 3. Develop & Implement Customer Research Plan 4. Translate Customer Needs to Product or Service CTQ's 5. Specify Targets, Tolerance Limits & Sigma Targets
Explore	1. Develop Product/Service Necessary Functions 2. Develop Conceptual Product/Service Designs 3. Develop High-Level Production Processes 4. Predict Capability & Evaluate Gaps
Design	1. Develop Detailed Product & Service Designs 2. Develop Detailed Production Process 3. Refine Capability & Gap Evaluation, Perform Tradeoffs 4. Develop Process Control & Validation Plans
Validate	1. Build Pilot Processes 2. Validate Pilot Readiness 3. Perform Pilot Testing 4. Analyze Gaps, Determine Root Causes 5. Evaluate Scale-up Potential 6. Develop Implementation & Transition Plans
Implement	1. Build Full-Scale Processes, Train Staff 2. Perform Start-up Testing 3. Analyze Gaps, Determine Root Causes 4. Transition to Process Owners 5. Evaluate & Close Design Project

*Just as in the case of "DMAIIC" in which an "I" (for "Implement") was added to the more familiar GE-based acronym "DMAIC", "DMEDVI" differs from GE's "DMADV" in that "E" (for "Explore") replaces "A" (for "Analyze") and "I" (for "Implement") is again added. "Implement" was added in both cases to place a stronger emphasis on the critical piloting step. "Explore" seems to be more appropriate language for a design process than "Analyze." The processes are very similar with slightly different points of emphasis.

(*The DMEDVI steps and sub-steps are based on material provided by Premier Performance Network, LLC)

The Leverage of DFSS

Ultimately, DFSS must become an integral part of any Six Sigma implementation because of its unbeatable ROI. This is based on the fact that DFSS identifies and tests a design concept and its process parameters against CTQ's *before* its release to production.

In the research paper, *Six Sigma in the Engineering Design Process* (American Statistical Association Quality and Productivity Research Conference, 1999), Gavin Finn dramatically illustrated the cost impact of the DFSS approach.

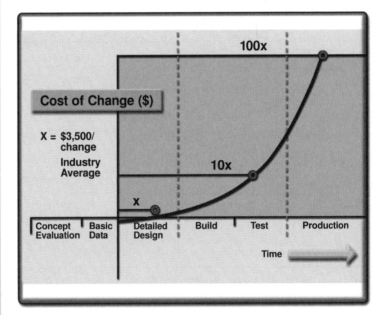

If DFSS can cause just a *single* design change to be made in the engineering phase, it can prevent a $3,500 design change (the industry average) from becoming a $35,000 change order (post-release, but before full-scale production), or even a $350,000 product re-design (during regular production). The following chart shows the potential impact of this cost structure (and therefore DFSS) since the majority of design changes occur *after* a design has been released to the Build and Test phase of product development.

Intro

Ready ?

6 Months

Project

Long Haul

DMAIC

Tools

R & R

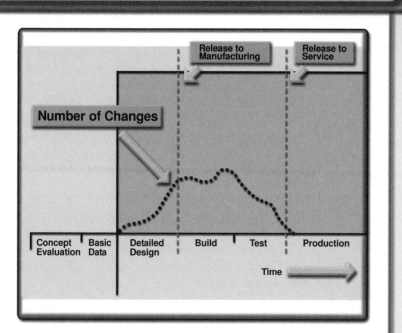

It will take only a few DFSS success stories to convince skeptics that Six Sigma is a complete proactive, business-planning tool and not "just" a reactive improvement process.

Spillover Lessons...

More important lessons are found in their entirety "behind" this main page. Click on any Lesson # to view them.

Lesson #3 – *Implement a Balanced Scorecard system with full deployment of metrics.*

Lesson #4 – *Create the process and systems for learning and growth.*

The Check List:

Have you...

❏ Identified ways to aim Six Sigma at increasingly strategic organizational issues?

❏ Created an aggressive plan to get the most out of the cadre of current Black Belts and Green Belts?

❏ Budgeted significant funds to train and support Green Belts throughout the organization?

❏ Examined and aligned management systems (e.g., Promotion, Reward & Recognition, Personal Performance and Operations Reviews, Communications & Organizational Learning) to support Six Sigma thinking and behavior?

❏ Committed to incorporating Six Sigma thinking and behavior into your own management style?

❏ Created excitement about a Six Sigma future?

Intro

Ready ?

6 Months

Project

Long Haul

DMAIIC

Tools

R & R

Chapter 6:
Six Sigma Survival Kit

Disciplined and data driven approach to process improvement... or tips, tools and techniques to survive a project!

Purpose of this chapter:

To present the Six Sigma methodology that puts people with knowledge and experience to work in teams to systematically analyze and solve problems improving process performance, project-by-project.

For senior executives and managers this chapter...

- Provides the six major steps, sub-steps, and recommended tools to use to guide a team through the DMAIIC model.

The Big Picture:

What is the Six Sigma Methodology?

Dr. Deming reintroduced the world in 1950 to the scientific method known as the <u>Plan-Do-Check-Act (PDCA) Cycle</u>, also known as the <u>Deming Cycle</u> for continuous improvement.

However, it is the "CAPDo" cycle that is the heart of <u>Process Management</u>. It simply means that daily improvement starts with a "check" on performance, which uncovers

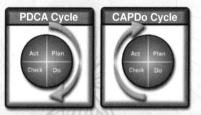

"gaps" that need to be filled. "PDCA" is used when a new product, process, or service is first developed; eventually becomes part of an ongoing Process Management and CAPDo cycle.

The PDCA/CAPDo cycle has been translated into a practical 6-step approach for teams to use during their problem solving/process improvement efforts. Improvement projects can now incorporate the disciplined process called DMAIIC (pronounced de-MAY-ic):

Design, **M**easure, **A**nalyze, **I**mprove, **I**mplement, **C**ontrol.

The DMAIIC model is an extension of the PDCA/CAPDo Cycle

Steps*	PDCA Equivalent	Purpose	Sub steps*
Define	*Check* to find a process in need of improvement	Select an appropriate project and define the problem, especially in terms of customer-critical demands	a. Qualify the project b. Determine project approach c. Define outcomes. d. Identify stakeholders e. Select team f. Launch the project g. Create project plan
Measure	*Check* current performance	Gain information about process performance and develop a problem statement	a. Define the current process b. Address "low-hanging fruit" c. Confirm key customer requirements d. Gather initial data and determine current performance e. Stratify data f. Establish cost benefit g. Develop problem statement & project scorecard
Analyze	*Act* to analyze gaps	Analyze the causes of the problem and verify suspected root cause(s)	a. Develop cause and effect hypotheses b. Gather causal data c. Determine and validate root causes
Improve	*Act* to develop changes to the Plan	Identify actions to reduce defects and variation caused by root cause(s) and plan the implementation of selected actions	a. Identify breakthroughs b. Select practical approaches c. Perform cost/benefit analysis d. Design future state e. Establish performance targets f. Further develop project scorecard
Implement	*Do* the changes, Check the results	Implement the plan. Evaluate the measurable improvement (if not evident, return to step one)	a. Gain approval to implement b. Train c. Execute d. Measure results e. Develop control methods f. Manage change
Control	*Act* to incorporate successful changes in the Plan	Control the process to ensure continued, improved performance; determine if improvements can be transferred elsewhere; identify lessons learned and next steps; celebrate!	a. Report scorecard data b. Create process control plan c. Apply P-D-C-A process d. Identify replication opportunities e. Develop future plans

* DMAIIC steps and sub steps are based on work provided by Premier Performance Network, LLC

The DMAIIC Steps, Tools, and Tips

Define: a. Qualify the Project

PURPOSE:

To initiate action addressing an identified problem through a team problem-solving process.

TOOLS TO USE:

Typical: The strategic plan and historical process performance data.

THE CHECK LIST:

Have you...

- ☐ As <u>process owner</u>, decided to act on an identified problem that integrates with your goals?
- ☐ Assured the problem is an important one to tackle based upon:
  - Its level of complexity?
  - Its financial impact?
  - Whether its root cause is known or unknown?
- ☐ Linked the problem directly to improved customer satisfaction?
- ☐ Identified the scale of financial and human resources that will likely be required to solve the problem?
- ☐ Committed to providing all of the resources needed to make the project a success?

Define: b. Determine project approach

PURPOSE:

To make sure that the right people are taking the most efficient and effective route to fixing the problem(s) at hand.

TOOLS TO USE:

Typical: None.

THE CHECK LIST:

Have you...

- ☐ Chosen to take management action when you know that the level of customer concern is high, the available resources are adequate and that there are effective solutions to known causes?

THE DEFINE STEP

Tools to Use:
"*Typical*": use to get started.
"*Optional*": additional or advanced tools for deeper process knowledge.

The Check List details things your team needs to do before moving on to the next step/sub step.

Intro

Ready?

6 Months

Project

Long Haul

DMAIIC

Tools

R & R

❑ Made individual assignments when the problem requires an intense application of specialized knowledge?

❑ Selected a DMAIIC <u>project team</u> approach when the possible causes, required knowledge and likely solutions are spread throughout an entire process.

❑ Set aggressive goals backed by realistic resources and authority?

Define: c. Define outcomes

PURPOSE:

To make the case that a problem be addressed and the process improved.

TOOLS TO USE:

Typical:

Affinity Diagram (see pg.192)	Identifies "good reasons to fix the problem."
Brainstorming	Generates lots of ideas.
Force Field Analysis	Identifies the drivers and roadblocks to successful problem resolution.

THE CHECK LIST:

Have you…

❑ Stated the size and importance of the "performance gap" in terms of potential dollars saved or additional revenue generated?

• What level of performance is required?

• Where is the performance now?

• What is the level of urgency?

• Are there related issues to be addressed?

❑ Confirmed the impact of the improvement with data and customer input?

Don't forget that the outcomes should trace back to the customer.

Define: d. Identify stakeholders

PURPOSE:

To identify those who may be involved in solving the problem.

TOOLS TO USE:

Typical: None

Intro

Ready ?

6 Months

Project

Long Haul

DMAIIC

Tools

R & R

THE CHECK LIST:

Have you...

- ❑ Considered everyone who might have a stake in seeing the problem addressed?:
  - Customers?
  - People who work with the process?
  - Suppliers?
  - The Boss?
  - Process links, e.g., support process owners?
  - Shareholders?
- ❑ Identified the stakeholders biggest concerns regarding:
  - Cost?
  - Timing?
  - Resource requirements and availability?
  - Control?
  - Job security?
- ❑ Identified the best way to involve stakeholders in the project?

Define: e. Select the team

PURPOSE:

To select a team that has the right people, power, performance parameters and passion to create solutions that work.

TOOLS TO USE:

Typical:

Responsibility Flow Chart (see pg. 201)	• Aligns people/functions within the framework of "the big picture." • Identifies the most critical relationships to improve or maintain
Project Charter Worksheet	• Records the expectations of both the organization and the team. • Clarifies the project's scope and resources, enabling the team's work to be focused and realistic.

THE CHECK LIST:

Have you...

- ❑ Created a team project charter which CLEARLY communicates the definition of project success to EVERY team member?
- ❑ Confirmed the responsibilities of every team role (sponsor, leader, etc.) both with the person filling it and the team including:

Don't rely on memory... write it all down.

- Team Sponsor?   • Lead team?
- Team Leader?   • Black Belt?
- Members?

❑ Been realistic about resources and aggressive about targets?
❑ Clarified team support resources?
  • Who might be needed to provide information?

Define: f. Launch the Project

PURPOSE:

To design and conduct a first meeting that begins to build a solid team and an aggressive project plan.

TOOLS TO USE:

Typical:

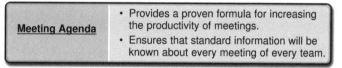

| **Meeting Agenda** | • Provides a proven formula for increasing the productivity of meetings.
• Ensures that standard information will be known about every meeting of every team. |

THE CHECK LIST:

Have you...

❑ Communicated clear expectations to ALL of the people who have accepted team roles?
❑ Set aside a minimum of two hours to build both the team and the project plan?
❑ Included a process to develop a Team-Behavior Contract to define how you will deal with tough issues, decisions and each other?
❑ Taken care of meeting logistics:
  • Comfortable meeting space?
  • Meeting equipment (Flip charts, Post-its, etc.)?
  • Project materials (Supporting data, Project Charter, etc.)?
  • Meeting notices?
  • Line coverage, if needed?
❑ Developed the plan to communicate the results of ALL meetings to ALL of the project stakeholders?
❑ Created a meeting agenda that gets the entire team involved and excited about the project?

Intro

Ready ?

6 Months

Project

Long Haul

DMAIIC

Tools

R & R

Define: g. Create a project plan

PURPOSE:

To create a single document that records both the proposed and actual execution of your team's <u>project plan</u>.

TOOLS TO USE:

Typical:

Project Planning Worksheet	• Provides a complete picture of the team and its work. • Allows the team to monitor its performance against a plan.

Optional: <u>Affinity Diagram</u>, <u>Responsibility Matrix</u>, <u>Contingency Planning/PDPC</u>, <u>Tree Diagram</u>, <u>GANTT Chart</u>

THE CHECK LIST:

Have you...

❏ Reinforced your project's "business case" in order to keep everyone focused and energized?

❏ Matched the frequency of your meetings with the pace of the work of your project?

❏ Completed and distributed the Project Planning Worksheet?

Don't bury performance gaps; instead make them highly visible so they'll get addressed.

Measure: a. Define the current process

THE MEASURE STEP

PURPOSE:

To create an accurate picture of how work is currently done.

TOOLS TO USE:

Typical:

Responsibility Flow Chart (see pg. 201)	• Shows the "hand-offs" that create complexity and process problems.

Optional: <u>Flow Chart</u>, <u>Process Profile</u>, <u>Process Inventory</u>, <u>Layout Diagrams</u>, <u>Process Watch</u>

THE CHECK LIST:

Have you...

❏ Involved the people who work IN the process as well as those who designed it?

❏ Developed a realistic picture of the current process?

Come to agreement about how the work is ACTUALLY done. This is NOT a game of "let's pretend"!

Intro

Ready ?

6 Months

Project

Long Haul

DMAIIC

Tools

R & R

❑ Involved all of the stakeholders in the process?
❑ Reviewed and validated the "final" <u>Flow Chart</u>?

Measure: b. Address "low-hanging fruit"

PURPOSE:

To tackle problems that can be easily identified, based on process knowledge and experience, rather than on a detailed analysis of the process.

TOOLS TO USE:

Typical:

Process Deficiency Worksheet	A simple way to compare the impact and difficulty level of tackling different pieces of "low-hanging fruit."

Optional: <u>Process Map or Flow Chart</u>, <u>Check Sheet</u>, <u>Run Chart</u>, <u>Pareto Chart</u>, <u>Responsibility Flow Chart</u>, <u>Process Management Charts</u>

THE CHECK LIST:

Have you...

❑ Thought first of unnecessary activities that add only time and not value for the customer?
❑ Looked at anything done or handled more than once?
❑ Eliminated the obvious "dumb stuff" that finds its way into every process?
❑ Involved all team members in identifying the process problems that occur repeatedly?
❑ Viewed the process "through the eyes of your customer"?

Measure: c. Confirm Key Customer Requirements (KCR)

PURPOSE:

To focus improvement efforts on those parts of the process that have a significant impact on what matters most to the customer.

No matter how small, every little thing counts when combined with other improvements.

TOOLS TO USE:

Typical:

Customer Requirements Table	Shows examples of Key Customer Requirements within some standard categories.

Optional: Customer Prioritization Table, Customer Interview Guide

THE CHECK LIST:

Have you...

- ❑ Identified the needs of both internal and external customers, *but* made sure to prioritize both categories of your customers *and* their needs?
- ❑ Talked to your most critical customers repeatedly? Requirements change and so should your process. Keep an ongoing dialog with your customer.
- ❑ Made the KCR's *measurable* so that the performance of your process can be evaluated *objectively?*

Measure: d. Gather initial data & determine current performance

PURPOSE:

To see how well (or poorly) you're now doing in the process variables that have the biggest impact on key customer requirements.

TOOLS TO USE:

Typical:

Check Sheet	Often makes patterns visible by the simple acts of counting and recording.
Run Chart	Displays trends in performance data over time.

Optional: Nominal Group Technique (NGT), Check Sheet, Gage R&R Study, Process Capability Analysis, Cycle-Time Analysis, Customer Requirements Table

Ready ?

6 Months

Project

Long Haul

DMAIIC

Tools

R & R

Intro

Ready ?

6 Months

Project

Long Haul

DMAIIC

Tools

R & R

THE CHECK LIST:

Have you...

❑ Chosen measures that accurately assess what matters to the *prime* process stakeholders?

❑ Measured both *results* (outcome indicators and key process *"alarms"* (upstream indicators)

❑ Rated process performance based on data, not opinion?
- Use data-based tools to help the team see and interpret current process performance.
- Don't use a tool more complicated than the problem it's aimed at solving.

❑ Tracked process performance over a time period that's representative of your business?

Measure: e. Stratify Data

PURPOSE:

To break down your process data into smaller groups in order to find the most significant contributors to the performance gap.

TOOLS TO USE:

Typical:

Pareto Chart (see pg. 200)	Displays the 20% of the sub-processes that are causing 80% of the performance gap.
Histogram (see pg. 199)	Provides a "snapshot" of the current Centering, Variability, and Shape of your process data.
Control Charts (see pg.192)	Identifies built-in variation in your process, as well as "special causes" that must be removed before the process can be made predictable.
Sigma Conversion Table (see pg. 203)	Expresses current process performance in terms of Sigma levels.

Optional: Run, Check Sheet, Process Capability Analysis, Gage R&R Study, Cycle-Time Analysis, Scatter Diagram, Customer Requirements Table, Contingency Table Analysis

Intro

Ready ?

6 Months

Project

Long Haul

DMAIIC

Tools

R & R

THE CHECK LIST:
Have you...

❑ Broken down your data to reveal the "vital few" processes that are causing most of your performance gap?
   - Do detailed statistical analysis only on the <u>vital few</u> contributors to the process performance gap.
   - A simple <u>Pareto Chart</u> is the best tool for this job.
❑ Uncovered the amount of variation that's built into your process(es)?
   - Assume that <u>variation</u> exists in all data. Dig deeper into your "vital few" problem areas to get an accurate picture of the variation within them.
   - <u>Histograms</u> present a clear and powerful snapshot of your process variation.
   - Don't "<u>tamper</u>" (random changes unsupported by data) with a process. Unless you're lucky, it usually creates more variation AND higher costs.
❑ Determined whether your process(es) is capable of meeting your customer's specifications?
   - <u>Specification limits</u> are measures of the customer's needs. First find the real "capability" of your problem processes... then keep improving them until you meet or exceed their needs.
   - Answer the basic question, "Are these problem processes '<u>in control</u>'?" If they are, then they will have *predictable* results. If not, any process improvements will have *unpredictable* results.
   - Don't think that a process is "predictable" (in statistical control) just because it's "capable" (able to meet specs).
❑ Translated your current performance into a comparable "Sigma-level"?
   - Once you've taken the first step of expressing your current "<u>defect rate</u>" into an equivalent "Sigma-performance," don't get depressed...it's a baseline, NOT an indictment.
   - Take a few minutes to brainstorm the impact of creating <u>6 Sigma Processes</u> that will average 3.4 defects/million opportunities vs typical results of 7,000-67,000 defects/million opportunities.

Intro

Ready ?

6 Months

Project

Long Haul

DMAIIC

Tools

R & R

• Don't try to take EVERY process to a 6 Sigma level. It will be a daily challenge to bring (and maintain) just your "vital few" processes to that level of excellence.

Measure: f. Establish $ benefits

PURPOSE:

To translate the benefits of the improvement project into the most tangible and powerful terms of all: increased profits from lower costs and/or increased revenues.

TOOLS TO USE:

Typical:

Cost Factors Check List/ Cost-Analysis Worksheets	Includes the most common costs that result from poor quality and under-performing processes.

Optional: Process Capability Analysis

THE CHECK LIST:

Have you...

❑ Produced cost and revenue figures that your finance people support?
  • Get help from your Finance and Accounting department to ensure that the ROI figures are accurate AND believable.
  • Don't overstate the potential financial impact of the improvement. People can smell a sales pitch.
❑ Clearly stated the benefits of the proposed improvement project that people are interested (even excited) to tackle it?
  • Know and respect your audience. Be sure that you can easily connect their work with the projected benefits.

> *Express the financial impact in ways other than just cost-cutting terms. Tell people how the improvement will help the business grow!*

Measure: g. Develop a problem statement & project scorecard

PURPOSE:

To clearly state the "what, where, when" and "how much" of a proposed improvement project.

Intro

Ready ?

6 Months

Project

Long Haul

DMAIIC

Tools

R & R

Tools to Use:
Typical:

Problem Statement Check List	Guidelines for creating a problem statement that clarifies the project & energizes the team.
Affinity Diagram (see pg. 192)	Allows the key parts of a problem to emerge naturally from the data that's gathered and the knowledge of the team members.
Project Scorecard	A helpful tool for tracking and communicating a Six Sigma team's process improvement plans, actions, and results.

The Check List:
Have you...

❑ Made the "business case" for the problem?
  • All stakeholders should easily understand the statement.
❑ Clearly communicated the essence of the problem and the impact of the solution?
  • Always state directly how the problem and its solution affect the key performance measures of the organization.
  • State the impact of the problem in measurable terms.
  • Communicate that the problem is *significant* (worth solving), yet *solvable* over a fairly short period of time.
❑ Created a positive and challenging start for the team?
  • Don't suggest a possible cause or potential solution of the problem. Let the real cause and solution emerge naturally based on the team's analyses.
  • Describe what's happening in the process as it's currently performed rather than assigning blame to an individual.
❑ Recorded your teams name, problem statement, and preliminary data onto your team's project scorecard?

Analyze: a. Develop cause & effect hypotheses

THE ANALYZE STEP

Purpose:
To determine what is causing the problem by focusing on the causal relationships between those factors (causes) that contribute to the variation in a process (effect).

TOOLS TO USE:

Typical:

| **Flow Chart** (see pg. 199) | To review how work is done and identifies potential problem areas. |
| **Brainstorming** | Generate lots of ideas as to possible causes. |

THE CHECK LIST:

Have you...

☐ Solicited input on potential causes from all team members?
  • Analysis is a search for causes. Identify causes focusing on those that significantly contribute to the problem—the <u>root causes</u>.
  • If you don't involve the right people—those with current knowledge and experience in the current problem area of the process—your initial cause and effect "hypotheses" may lead you in the wrong direction.

☐ Directed the team's thinking to examine potential causes related to people, policies, procedures, equipment, material, or environment?
  • Determine your outcome objectives. This will provide clues as to where to begin identifying causes.

Analyze: b. Gather causal data

PURPOSE:

To gather and organize data that will later help isolate and validate the root cause(s).

TOOLS TO USE:

Typical:

Affinity (see pg. 192)	Allows free-thinking of causes to emerge and begin to define natural grouping.
Cause & Effect Diagram (see pg. 192)	To provide an integrated picture of all possible causes identified by the different team members.
5 Whys	Asking "why" five times to get to the root cause of a problem.
Process Deficiency Worksheet	To identify typical process deficiencies after mapping a process and target those that can be addressed with a quick fix.

Intro | Ready? | 6 Months | Project | Long Haul | DMAIIC | Tools | R & R

Optional: <u>The 5 S's</u>, <u>Failure to Follow Analysis</u>, <u>Twenty Questions</u>, <u>Cycle-Time Analysis</u>, <u>Gage R&R Study</u>, <u>Critical Pathways Analysis (AND)</u>, <u>Taguchi Methods</u>, <u>Design of Experiments (DOE)</u>, <u>Failure Mode & Effect Analysis (FMEA)</u>

THE CHECK LIST:

Have you...

❑ Identified typical deficiencies for quick fixes or further analysis?
  - Begin with experience-based guesses and progress toward databased analysis.

❑ Identified causes by analyzing the data your team already has or by experimentation?
  - Begin with experience-based guesses and progress toward databased analysis.If not part of the team, help the people gathering the data to understand how the data will be used. This will go a long way in data integrity.

> *Generate as many causes as possible. Subsequent validation of the causes will help reduce the size of the list.*

Analyze: c. Determine & validate root causes

PURPOSE:

To select the root cause(s) that the team will focus their improvement efforts on through the rest of the project.

TOOLS TO USE:

Typical:

Check Sheet	Simple record keeping of the occurrences of causes.
Pareto Chart (see pg. 200)	Prioritizes the causes that contribute to the problem.
Run Chart	Displays trends in performance data over time.

Optional: <u>Histogram</u>, <u>Control Charts</u>, <u>Process Capability Analysis</u>, <u>Scatter Diagram</u>, <u>Interrelationship Digraph (ID)</u>, <u>Design of Experiments (DOE)</u>

> *Don't focus on solving the problem yet! This is still about identifying THE root cause(s).*

THE CHECK LIST:

Have you...

❑ Made sure the team has verified a root cause?
  - Team knowledge and experience can go a long way in selecting root causes. Gathering additional data will make

Intro
Ready ?
6 Months
Project
Long Haul
DMAIIC
Tools
R & R

THE
IMPROVE
STEP

certain that the team's assumptions are correct.

• If the data from simple tools do not help validate a root cause, consider experimentation.

Improve: a. Identify breakthroughs

PURPOSE:

To identify creative solutions that will significantly (not incrementally) improve the problem.

TOOLS TO USE:

Typical:

Brainstorming	Generates lots of ideas of possible countermeasures to root cause(s).
Benchmarking	Gather ideas from others who are doing the same work.
Affinity Diagram (see pg. 192)	Allows freethinking of countermeasures to emerge and begin to define natural grouping
Interrelationship Digraph	Look at cause and effect relationships that exist between countermeasures.

Optional: Quality Function Deployment (QFD), Creativity Methods (e.g. Imaginary Brainstorming, DeBono's Thinking Hats, etc.)

THE CHECK LIST:

Have you...

❑ Stimulated the team's thinking through creativity exercises before identifying breakthroughs.

- Go for quantity! The more countermeasures you come up with, the better the likelihood of one that works the best.

- For really big breakthroughs, push the team to develop uniquely different countermeasures. Creativity methods are especially helpful in overcoming the "same old way of doing things."

- Learn from others. Benchmarking is a great way to study how others solved the same problem. BUT, adapt it to your specific situation.

Don't allow negative reactions to ideas stop the thinking process.

Intro

Ready ?

6 Months

Project

Long Haul

DMAIIC

Tools

R & R

Improve: b. Select practical approaches

PURPOSE:

To identify those approaches that will most significantly reduce or eliminate the root cause(s).

TOOLS TO USE:

Typical:

Countermeasures Check List	Criteria to help select the best approaches.
Contingency Planning - (PDPC)	Identifies likely problems that can occur and the possible responses to fixing those problems.

Optional: Tree Diagram, Prioritization Matrices

THE CHECK LIST:

Have you...

❑ Evaluated the countermeasures against a set of criteria?
  • Some solutions may require multiple countermeasures to achieve significant improvements.
  • Don't forget "Murphy's Law." Anticipate things that can go wrong and eliminate those approaches that might have too many barriers to overcome.

Improve: c. Perform cost-benefit analysis

PURPOSE:

To identify the financial impact of a selected improvement approach.

TOOLS TO USE:

Typical:

Cost-Benefit Analysis/Future Rate of Return	Establishes the net financial benefit of a selected approach.

THE CHECK LIST:

Have you...

❑ Considered all the internal failure costs and external failure costs to meet customer requirements?
  • Financial Analysis is another way of selecting the best

Intro

Ready?

6 Months

Project

Long Haul

DMAIIC

Tools

R & R

approach. If the net financial benefit is insufficient, look for another approach.

- Doing a cost-benefit analysis is a useful way to establish priorities and plan for resource requirements.
- Use the simple formula:

Estimated Financial Benefit – *Estimated Investment* = *Estimated Net Financial Benefit*

Improve: d. Design future state

PURPOSE:

To design the most efficient and effective work process that includes the identified countermeasures to the causes of the problem.

TOOLS TO USE:

Typical:

Brainstorming	Generates lots of possible improvement ideas.
Flow Chart (see pg. 199)	Create a diagram of what the improved process would look like.
Action Plan Worksheet	Identifies activities and assigns accountability when implementing the countermeasures.
Affinity Diagram (see pg. 192)	Allows freethinking of countermeasures to emerge to define natural groupings.

Optional: Countermeasure Evaluation Check Sheet, Tree Diagram, Contingency Planning - (PDPC), Design of Experiments (DOE), Benchmarking

THE CHECK LIST:

Have you...

❑ Reviewed the Flow Chart?
- Draw a picture of what the "ideal" process should look like. This will be a helpful document to pass around to others who work with the process to review and critique.
- Incorporate ideas from others to help facilitate their "buy-in" later on when the process is changed.

❑ Made sure that your selected countermeasures are part of your implementation plan?

Don't make any changes to the process before your Action Plan is developed. This ensures your final results are based on your actions?

© 2001 Brassard & Ritter, LLC

Intro
Ready ?
6 Months
Project
Long Haul
DMAIIC
Tools
R & R

Improve: e. Establish performance targets

PURPOSE:

To establish the level of performance needed for the process to operate well.

TOOLS TO USE:

Typical:

| **Benchmarking** | Gather ideas from others who are doing the same work. |

Optional: Quality Function Deployment

THE CHECK LIST:

Have you...

- ❑ Benchmarked others?
- ❑ Set performance guidelines (long-term and intermediate) based on what others are doing as well as what you need from your process?

Improve: f. Further develop project scorecard

PURPOSE:

To track and communicate the effectiveness of your actions to improve the process.

TOOLS TO USE:

Typical:

Check Sheet	Often makes patterns visible by the simple acts of counting and recording.
Run Chart	Displays trends in performance data over time.
Pareto Chart (see pg. 200)	Displays the 20% of the sub-processes that are causing 80% of the performance gap.
Histogram (see pg. 199)	Provides a "snapshot" of the current Centering, Variability, and Shape of your process data.
Control Charts (see pg. 192)	Identifies built-in variation in your process, as well as "special causes" that must be removed before the process can be made predictable.
Process Capability Analysis (see pg. 200)	Measures how well, or capable your process is in meeting your customer's requirements.

Intro

Ready ?

6 Months

Project

Long Haul

DMAIIC

Tools

R & R

Optional: <u>Gage R&R Study</u>, <u>Cycle-Time Analysis</u>, <u>Scatter Diagram</u>, <u>Failure Mode and Effect Analysis (FMEA)</u>.

THE CHECK LIST:

Have you...

❑ Made sure your Project Scorecard completely and clearly tracks progress of you process improvement actions and measures?

❑ Distributed the scorecard to those that need to see it?

THE
IMPLEMENT
STEP

Implement: a. Gain approval to implement

PURPOSE:

To make a formal presentation to management to request approval for a trial or full implementation of your improvement plan.

TOOLS TO USE:

Typical:

Project Planning Worksheet	• Provides a complete picture of the team and its work. • Allows the team to monitor its performance against a plan.
Responsibility Flow Chart (see pg. 201)	• Shows the "hand-offs" that create complexity and process problems.
Cost-Benefit Analysis/Future Rate of Return	Establishes the net financial benefit of a selected approach.

Optional: <u>Process Map</u>, <u>Responsibility Matrix</u>, <u>GANTT Chart</u>, <u>Tree Diagram</u>, <u>Contingency Planning</u>

THE CHECK LIST:

Have you...

❑ Planned the presentation?

• Use your project charter, plan, and scorecard in your presentation.

❑ Demonstrated that the team worked effectively together both in the team project AND the team presentation.

• Answer questions about the meeting logistics and the presentation content.

Intro

Ready ?

6 Months

Project

Long Haul

DMAIIC

Tools

R & R

Implement: b. Train

PURPOSE:

To train key personnel in the new or updated process.

TOOLS TO USE:

Typical:

Implementation Training Matrix	Identifies who needs to be trained and to what level (or depth) of knowledge they need to do the work.
Responsibility Flow Chart (see pg. 201)	• Shows the "hand-offs" that create complexity and process problems.

Optional: Flow Chart, Process Map, Process Profiling, Process Inventory, Customer Requirements Table, Layout Diagrams, Process Deficiency Worksheet, Responsibility Matrix, GANTT Chart, Project Plan, Benchmarking

THE CHECK LIST:

Have you...

❑ Identified what training is needed?
  • The most effective way to get people to accept change is to include them in the change process. Include them as early as possible and solicit their recommendations.
❑ Made sure that everyone that needs to be trained, has been trained?
  • Make sure that the training is applied. Share not only what they need to do differently, but why.
❑ Planned for follow-up after the training?
  • Support people after the training. Have some familiar with the planned changed available on-the-job to reinforce what was learned in training.

Implement: c. Execute

PURPOSE:

To ensure successful implementation through careful planning and leadership.

TOOLS TO USE:

Typical: Knowledge, Experience and Wisdom

Intro

Ready ?

6 Months

Project

Long Haul

DMAIIC

Tools

R & R

THE CHECK LIST:

Have you...

- ❑ Planned an effective communication campaign: Who needs to know? What they need to know? How often they need to know?
- ❑ Provided effective leadership?
- ❑ Provided necessary support through the changes?

Implement: d. Measure results

PURPOSE:

To monitor the implementation plan and make sure everything is going according to plan.

TOOLS TO USE:

Typical:

Check Sheet	Often makes patterns visible by the simple acts of counting and recording.
Run Chart	Displays trends in performance data over time
Pareto Chart (see pg. 200)	Displays the 20% of the sub-processes that are causing 80% of the performance gap.
Histogram (see pg. 199)	Provides a "snapshot" of the current Centering, Variability, and Shape of your process data.
Control Charts (see pg. 192)	Identifies built-in variation in your process, as well as "special causes" that must be removed before the process can be made predictable.
Process Capability Analysis (see pg. 200)	Measures how well, or capable your process is in meeting your customer's requirements.

Optional: Optional: Gage R&R Study, Cycle-Time Analysis, Scatter Diagram, Failure Mode and Effect Analysis (FMEA), Customer Requirements Table

THE CHECK LIST:

Have you...

- ❑ Verified that the materials, training, and support are carried out as intended?

Intro

Ready ?

6 Months

Project

Long Haul

DMAIIC

Tools

R & R

❑ Reviewed indicators affecting KCR's?
  - Collect and analyze data in the same manner as you did in the *Measure* and *Analyze* steps. This assures consistency in comparing before and after (or achieving desired) changes in the process' performance.
❑ Documented any necessary modifications to the plan?
  - Be open to modifying the plan, even the best-laid plans can go astray. Make sure you document any changes and learn from them to improve your future improvement planning.

Implement: e. Develop control methods

PURPOSE:

To sustain performance improvement by taking action to maintain the gains.

TOOLS TO USE:

Typical:

| The Process Book | A "book" containing all the useful information about a process including its objectives, methods, training, records, results, etc. |
| Process Management Charts | Charts organizing the who, what, when, where, why, and how of the process. |

THE CHECK LIST:

Have you…

❑ Identified actions necessary to ensure people are working within the process?
❑ Assembled and made available all information about a process that is necessary to best manage a process for ongoing performance?

Implement: f. Manage change

PURPOSE:

To help others gain acceptance to change.

Intro

Ready?

6 Months

Project

Long Haul

DMAIIC

Tools

R & R

THE
CONTROL
STEP

TOOLS TO USE:

Typical:

| **Change Management Checklist** | A list of key responsibilities when managing for change. |

THE CHECK LIST:

Have you...

❑ Helped others manage change?
  • Change is easier when you involve the stakeholders and team members in the change process from the beginning.
  • Work *with* your team members in providing the key elements for successful change: vision, skills, resources, action plan, and communication.

Control: a. Report scorecard data

PURPOSE:

To update the scorecard data to visually demonstrate the impact of the project's countermeasures.

TOOLS TO USE:

Typical:

| **Project Scorecard** | A helpful tool to track and communicate process improvement actions. |
| **The DMAIIC Story** | A summary of the use of the DMAIIC model. |

THE CHECK LIST:

Have you...

❑ Updated your charts to show current versus targeted performance?
❑ Indicated on the charts the effects of the countermeasures?
❑ Prepared to present at an Operational Review?

Control: b. Create process control plan

PURPOSE:

To create or revise a Process Control Plan

Intro

Ready ?

6 Months

Project

Long Haul

DMAIIC

Tools

R & R

TOOLS TO USE:

Typical:

The Process Book	A "book" containing all the useful information about a process including its objectives, methods, training, records, results, etc.
Process Management Charts	Charts organizing the who, what, when, where, why, and how of the process.

THE CHECK LIST:

Have you...

- ☐ Established a Process Control Plan?
  - If no, create one.
  - If yes, update the Flow Chart, change indicators or data collection plans, and response plan.

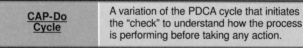

Control: c. P-D-C-A process

PURPOSE:

To continually improve the process using the Plan-Do-Check-Act-Cycle.

TOOLS TO USE:

Typical:

CAP-Do Cycle	A variation of the PDCA cycle that initiates the "check" to understand how the process is performing before taking any action.

THE CHECK LIST:

Have you...

- ☐ Checked the current process performance?
- ☐ Initiated action based on the current performance?
  - If the process is performing to plan, then standardize the activities by continuing to carry out the control plan.
  - If the process is not performing to plan, then initial a study to develop a new plan for improvement.

Intro

Ready ?

6 Months

Project

Long Haul

DMAIIC

Tools

R & R

Control: d. Identify replication opportunities

PURPOSE:

To create or revise a Process Control Plan

TOOLS TO USE:

Typical: None

THE CHECK LIST:

Have you...

- ❑ Made a commitment to support organizational learning?
- ❑ Developed a list of areas, departments, or even other processes that would benefit from your improvement work?
- ❑ Communicated your findings?

Control: e. Develop future plans

PURPOSE:

To reflect on your "lessons learned" and incorporate these into future projects.

TOOLS TO USE:

Typical: None

THE CHECK LIST:

Have you...

- ❑ Made a commitment to the never-ending pursuit of excellence and customer excitement?
- ❑ Identified your "lessons learned" including what you did well, and what you would do differently?
- ❑ Identified the next opportunity to be addressed to improve your process further?

Executives and Managers...

By learning and applying the Six Sigma methodology and tools, your people have begun to develop knowledge, experience, and dedication to their work, their team, and the organization. They have also systematically analyzed and solved critical problems that have led to improved process performance.

Take time to celebrate with them on all that they have learned and all that they have accomplished!

Intro

Ready ?

6 Months

Project

Long Haul

DMAIIC

Tools

R & R

Chapter 7:
Survival Tools

Data and information to make informed decisions

Purpose of this chapter:

To provide:

- Basic information on the most frequently used tools of the DMAIIC model, with more detail in the e-book.

- A list of advanced tools and other helpful topics that can be accessed through the e-book.

Expert Advice:

- Tools alone do not guarantee success. Likewise, teams alone do not guarantee success. But, it is the artful blending of the right individuals with their collective knowledge and experiences using the right tools that leads to higher levels of team effectiveness and success.

- The right people are those closest to the problem and process and, therefore, have the most knowledge about the problem and process.

- Clarify the issue(s); clearly and succinctly identify it and post it where everyone can see it.

- Use the tools to encourage dialog and sharing of knowledge between the team members. The tools are important, but real learning comes from exchanging ideas.

- Develop a <u>data collection plan</u> to get the most out of your data collection effort.

- Don't allow work to get lost; always keep it visible, making sure to post it on flip charts, pin boards, or walls.

  The tools are ways to document a team's thinking as well as to record minutes of meetings.

Most Frequently Used Tools

Affinity Diagram

What is it?

A graphic that organizes a large number of a team's ideas on an issue.

Construction Steps:

1. Define the issue; keep it neutral.
2. Generate lots of ideas; writing one idea per post-it.
3. Sort ideas as a team into natural, and new, groupings.
4. Summarize groups by writing a detailed header; descriptive headers should combine "action" and "purpose."

Cause & Effect Diagram

What is it?

A graphic tool to identify and organize all the possible causes that influence an outcome.

If "cause" categories aren't obvious, brainstorm the detail causes first, group them. and see which broad categories emerge.

Construction Steps:

1. Select the major "cause" categories and place in a diagram.
2. Brainstorm more detailed causes under each category; use the 5 Whys to dig deeper.
3. Analyze the chart for root cause(s).

Control Charts

What is it?

A graphic chart that monitors the centering and variation of a process and indicates whether the process is stable and in-control.

Construction Steps:

1. Select the appropriate control chart and collect 20-25 subgroups of data. Record data on a chart.
2. Calculate the appropriate statistics (average, variation, process average) and the control limits.
3. Draw the data points, centerline (process average), and upper and lower control limits.
4. Evaluate the process for stability and capability compared to customer needs.

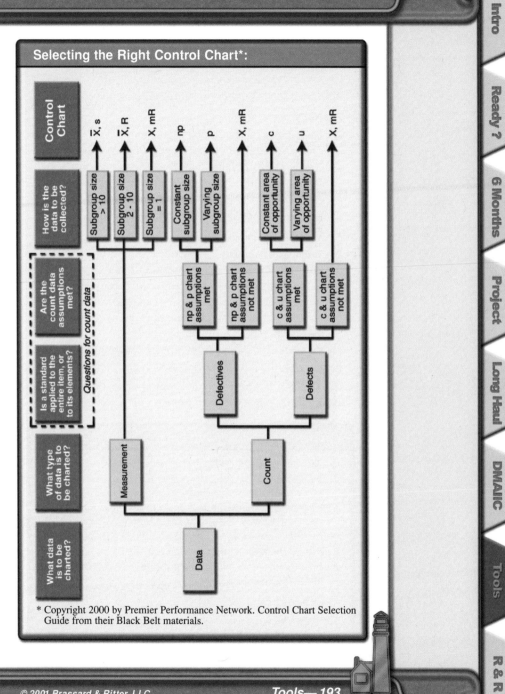

Selecting the Right Control Chart*:

| Control Chart | $\bar{X}$, s | $\bar{X}$, R | X, mR | np | p | X, mR | c | u | X, mR |

| How is the data to be collected? | Subgroup size > 10 | Subgroup size 2 - 10 | Subgroup size = 1 | Constant subgroup size | Varying subgroup size | | Constant area of opportunity | Varying area of opportunity |

Questions for count data

Are the count data assumptions met? — np & p chart assumptions met / np & p chart assumptions not met / c & u chart assumptions met / c & u chart assumptions not met

Is a standard applied to the entire item, or to its elements?

What type of data is to be charted? — Measurement — Count

Defectives — Defects

What data is to be charted? — Data

* Copyright 2000 by Premier Performance Network. Control Chart Selection Guide from their Black Belt materials.

Intro | Ready ? | 6 Months | Project | Long Haul | DMAIIC | Tools | R & R

Intro

Ready ?

6 Months

Project

Long Haul

DMAIIC

Tools

R & R

Interpreting Control Charts

- For easier assessment of Control Charts, draw the center line (that is, the process average) as a solid blue line, draw the upper and lower control limits as dashed red lines.

- A good process should be:
  (1) **Stable**; *that is, predictable and in control.*
      Determine stability by analyzing Control Charts for trends, shifts, or other out-of-control conditions (see below). Eliminate any special causes of <u>variation</u>.
  (2) **Capable**; *that is, able to meet customer requirements.*
      Use the <u>Histogram</u> or <u>Process Capability Analysis</u> to determine process capability.

- If a process is *not* stable or capable:
  (1) Implement process improvement efforts to shift the target to the desired level and/or reduce inherent variation.
  (2) Re-calculate the process mean, variation, and control limits based on new data. Update the control chart to reflect these new statistics and control limits.
  (3) Re-assess for stability and process capability.

- When a process *is* stable or capable, standardize the process. Use the new process mean and control limits on the chart, and continue monitoring the process.

Out-of-Control Conditions

1. Any single point outside the control limits.
2. Two of three consecutive points more than two sigma away from the center line.
3. Four of five points on the same side of and more than one sigma away from the center line.
4. A shift of seven or more consecutive points on either side of the center line.
5. A trend of seven consecutive points either increasing or decreasing.
6. Eight or more points that lie very close to the center line ("Hugging").
7. "Non-random" patterns that recur frequently.

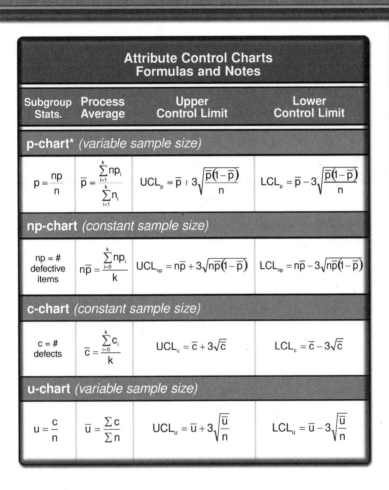

Attribute Control Charts
Formulas and Notes

Subgroup Stats.	Process Average	Upper Control Limit	Lower Control Limit
p-chart* *(variable sample size)*			
$p = \dfrac{np}{n}$	$\bar{p} = \dfrac{\sum_{i=1}^{k} np_i}{\sum_{i=1}^{k} n_i}$	$UCL_p = \bar{p} + 3\sqrt{\dfrac{\bar{p}(1-\bar{p})}{n}}$	$LCL_p = \bar{p} - 3\sqrt{\dfrac{\bar{p}(1-\bar{p})}{n}}$
np-chart *(constant sample size)*			
$np = \#$ defective items	$n\bar{p} = \dfrac{\sum_{i=0}^{k} np_i}{k}$	$UCL_{np} = n\bar{p} + 3\sqrt{n\bar{p}(1-\bar{p})}$	$LCL_{np} = n\bar{p} - 3\sqrt{n\bar{p}(1-\bar{p})}$
c-chart *(constant sample size)*			
$c = \#$ defects	$\bar{c} = \dfrac{\sum_{i=0}^{k} c_i}{k}$	$UCL_c = \bar{c} + 3\sqrt{\bar{c}}$	$LCL_c = \bar{c} - 3\sqrt{\bar{c}}$
u-chart *(variable sample size)*			
$u = \dfrac{c}{n}$	$\bar{u} = \dfrac{\sum c}{\sum n}$	$UCL_u = \bar{u} + 3\sqrt{\dfrac{\bar{u}}{n}}$	$LCL_u = \bar{u} - 3\sqrt{\dfrac{\bar{u}}{n}}$

Where:

np = # defective units

n = sample size within each subgroup

k = number of subgroups

*The p-chart formula creates changing upper and lower control limits for the varying sample sizes. Use a computer to draw these changing limits. Or, for a simplified approach, use the average sample size, n=Σn_i/k, for those samples within ±20% of n. For any samples exceeding ±20%, calculate the individual limits.

Intro

Ready ?

6 Months

Project

Long Haul

DMAIC

Tools

R & R

Intro

Ready ?

6 Months

Project

Long Haul

DMAIC

Tools

R & R

Variable Control Charts
Formulas, Factors, and Notes

Subgroup Statistics	Process Average	Upper Control Limit	Lower Control Limit

$\overline{X}$, R Chart

$\overline{X}$ Chart

$\overline{X} = \dfrac{\sum\limits_{j=1}^{n} X_j}{n}$	$\overline{\overline{X}} = \dfrac{\sum\limits_{i-1}^{k} \overline{X}_i}{k}$	$UCL_{\bar{x}} = \overline{\overline{X}} + A_2\overline{R}$	$LCL_{\bar{x}} = \overline{\overline{X}} - A_2\overline{R}$

R Chart

$R = X_{max} - X_{min}$	$\overline{R} = \dfrac{\sum\limits_{i-1}^{k} \overline{R}_i}{k}$	$UCL_R = D_4\overline{R}$	$LCL_R = D_3\overline{R}$

$\overline{X}$, s Chart

$\overline{X}$ Chart

$\overline{X} = \dfrac{\sum\limits_{j=1}^{k} X_j}{n}$	$\overline{\overline{X}} = \dfrac{\sum\limits_{i-1}^{k} \overline{X}_i}{k}$	$UCL_{\bar{x}} = \overline{\overline{X}} + A_3\overline{s}$	$LCL_{\bar{x}} = \overline{\overline{X}} - A_3\overline{s}$

s Chart

$s = \sqrt{\dfrac{\sum\limits_{j=1}^{n}(x_j - \overline{x})^2}{n-1}}$	$\overline{s} = \dfrac{\sum\limits_{i-1}^{k} s_i}{k}$	$UCL_S = B_4\overline{s}$	$LCL_S = B_3\overline{s}$

X, mR Chart

X Chart

Individual data points	$\overline{X} = \dfrac{\sum\limits_{i-1}^{k} \overline{X}_i}{k}$	$UCL_{\bar{x}} = \overline{X} + E_2\overline{R}$	$LCL_{\bar{x}} = \overline{X} - E_3\overline{R}$

mR Chart

$mR = \left|(X_{i+1} - X_i)\right|$	$\overline{R} = \dfrac{\sum\limits_{i-1}^{k-1} mR_i}{k-1}$	$UCL_{R_m} = D_4\overline{R}$	$LCL_{R_m} = D_3\overline{R}$

Where:

mR = moving range
s = subgroup standard deviation
n = sample size within each subgroup
k = number of subgroups
A2, A3, B3, B4, D3, D4, E2 = factors from the Table of Constants based on the subgroup sample size, n.

n	A_2	A_3	B_3	B_4	D_3	D_4	E_2
Table of Constants							
2	1.880	2.659	0	3.267	0	3.267	2.659
3	1.023	1.954	0	2.568	0	2.574	1.772
4	0.729	1.628	0	2.266	0	2.282	1.457
5	0.577	1.427	0	2.089	0	2.114	1.290
6	0.483	1.287	0.030	1.970	0	2.004	1.184
7	0.419	1.182	0.118	1.882	0.076	1.924	1.109
8	0.373	1.099	0.185	1.815	0.136	1.864	1.054
9	0.337	1.032	0.239	1.761	0.184	1.816	1.010
10	0.308	0.975	0.284	1.716	0.223	1.777	0.975

Notes

n=2 is the minimum sample size, since variation can only be calculated in samples greater than 1.

Intro   Ready ?   6 Months   Project   Long Haul   DMAIC   Tools   R & R

Design of Experiments

What is it?

A statistically designed study of the causal interrelationships of key variables to optimize new process design or improve current process performance.

Construction Steps:

1. Determine the purpose of the experiment.
2. Determine how the experiment's outcome is to be measured.
3. Identify the factors to be investigated and their levels.
4. Develop an experimental layout.
   - *Full factorial experiment*: studies all combinations of factors (variables) and levels (usually two: low and high). For example, a study that examines 3 factors at two levels is 2x2x2 or $2^3=8$ tests. If examining 5 factors at two levels you would have $2^5=64$ tests.
   - *Fractional factorial experiments*: As the number of factors increases, the number of tests required to study all main effects and interactions increases geometrically. For example, 10 factors would require $2^{10}=1024$ tests. This number of tests would require a prohibitive amount of resources (time, materials, personnel). In this case, use a fractional factorial experiment that uses fewer runs, e.g., screening, Plackett-Burman, response surface design.
5. Decide how many repetitions of the experiment are needed.
6. Order of the experiment randomly.
7. Conduct the experiments and measure their outcomes.
8. Analyze the experimental results.
9. Draw conclusions.
10. Perform confirming experiments.

Flow Chart/Process Map

What is it?

A graphic "map" of the sequence of steps and decisions carried out to produce an output (end product or service).

Construction Steps:

1. Select a process and decide where it begins and ends.
2. Determine its key steps and decision points.
3. Use symbols to draw the flow of the steps. Some simple ones to get started include:
   - An oval for start and end, as well as any inputs (materials, information or actions).
   - A box or rectangle to show a task or activity.
   - A diamond for a decision point.
   - A small circle with a number or letter in it to show continuation at another place on the page or to another page.
   - Arrows to show direction of the flow.
4. Have your team members and others review and finalize the Flow Chart.

Histogram

What is it?

A bar graph showing the <u>frequency distribution</u> of the process output, including centering and variation.

> The Histogram is a simple tool to see the capability of a process; that is, how well a process meets customer needs.

Construction Steps:

1. Decide on a process measure and collect data (try for at least 50-100 data points).
2. Complete/fill in a <u>frequency table</u>.
3. Draw a bar chart showing the centering and variation in the data.
4. Compare the distribution to customer needs:
   - Look for patterns in the Histogram indicating more than one data source. Stratify the data, if needed.
   - Determine whether the process meets your customer's needs? (Does the Histogram fall within the upper and lower specification?)

Intro

Ready ?

6 Months

Project

Long Haul

DMAIC

Tools

R & R

Pareto Chart

What is it?

A bar chart that ranks problems or issues to identify the most important one, thereby directing a team on what to address first or next.

By focusing on the vital few categories, a team will address roughly 80% of the problem.

Construction Steps:

1. Chose the problem or cause categories and associated unit of measures.

2. Select a time period and sort the gathered data into the categories.

3. Rank order the categories (most to least) and draw a bar graph with most on the left to least towards the right.

4. Interpret the chart.

Process Capability

What is it?

A concept, as well as measures, of how well a process's output (product or service) meets the requirements of the customer.

Construction Steps:

1. From your control chart, find the overall process average, $\bar{\bar{X}}$ and average range, $\bar{R}$ or standard deviation, s.

2. Identify the Upper Specification Limit (USL) and Lower Specification Limit (LSL) from your customer's requirement.

3. Calculate the estimated process standard deviation, $\hat{\sigma}$, based on the data from your control chart.

$$\hat{\sigma} = \bar{R}/d_2 \quad \text{or} \quad \hat{\sigma} = \bar{s}/c_4$$

Use the constants in the table at the right and where 'n' is the average subgroup size.

n	d_2	c_4
2	1.128	.798
3	1.693	.886
4	2.059	.922
5	2.326	.940
6	2.534	.952
7	2.794	.959
8	2.847	.965
9	2.970	.969
10	3.078	.973

4. Calculate a process capability index: *Inherent (simple) Process Capability Index, C_p:*

$$C_p = (USL - LSL)/6\hat{\sigma}$$

Interpretations of C_p:

- If $C_p<1$, indicates that a significant fraction of the process output is not meeting customer requirements.
- If $C_p=1$, then only about 3 in 1000 process outputs are not meeting customer requirements.
- If $C_p>1$, then there is a very small chance of the process outputs not meeting customer requirements.

Operational Process Capability Index, C_{pk}:

$$C_{pk} = Z_{min}/3$$

- For one-sided tolerance (only upper or lower specification limit):

$$Z_{min}= |\, SL - \bar{\bar{X}}\, |/\hat{\sigma}$$

where SL is the upper or lower specification.
- For two-sided tolerance interval calculates the smaller of the difference between the process average and the upper or lower specification:

$$Zmin= (USL - \bar{\bar{X}})/\hat{\sigma} \quad \text{or} \quad (\bar{\bar{X}} - USL)/\hat{\sigma}$$

- C_{pk} is similar in concept to the interpretations of the Inherent Process Capability, C_p.

Responsibility Flow Chart

What is it?
A Flow Chart variation that breaks a planning process into the sequence of tasks to be completed and aligns them under who has responsibility for the task.

Construction Steps:
1. Identify and list across a sheet of paper those people or departments that have responsibility for assigned tasks. List the job function rather than a person's name.
2. Identify the tasks to be accomplished and list in sequence under the responsible people/departments. In some cases more than one person/department may be responsible for a task.
3. Complete the diagram by drawing arrows showing the flow of the tasks.

Scatter Diagram

What is it?

A graphic chart clarifying the relationship that exists between two variables.

Construction Steps:

1. Choose variables to be correlated and collect (X, Y paired) data.
2. Draw an X-Y axis graph and plot the data points.
3. Interpret the graph.

Six Sigma

What is it?

A measure of a process's quality level.

Construction Steps:

      D=# Defects   U=# Units

      O=# Opportunities for a defect to occur

1. Calculate the total opportunities for a defect to occur:

   Total Opportunities = U x O

2. Calculate the defect rate (DPU):

   DPU = D/U

3. Calculate the defects per unit opportunity (DPO):

   DPO = DPU/O = D/(U x O)

4. Calculate the defects per million opportunities (DPMO):

   $DPMO = DPO \times 10^6$

5. Estimate the Long-Term Sigma value:

   Use the value from Step 4 and the Sigma Conversion Table on the next page to estimate the sigma value.

Tree Diagram

What is it?

A detailed breakdown of the assignable tasks necessary to accomplish a broad goal.

Sigma Conversion Table

Sigma	DPMO	Yield(%)	Sigma	DPMO	Yield(%)
6.0	3.4	99.99966	3.0	66,807	93.3
5.9	5.4	99.99946	2.9	80,757	91.9
5.8	8.5	99.99915	2.8	96,801	90.3
5.7	13	99.99866	2.7	115,070	88.5
5.6	21	99.9979	2.6	135,666	86.4
5.5	32	99.9968	2.5	158,655	84.1
5.4	48	99.9952	2.4	184,060	81.6
5.3	72	99.9928	2.3	211,855	78.8
5.2	108	99.9892	2.2	241,964	75.8
5.1	159	99.984	2.1	274,253	72.6
5.0	233	99.977	2.0	308,538	69.1
4.9	337	99.966	1.9	344,578	65.5
4.8	483	99.952	1.8	382,089	61.8
4.7	687	99.931	1.7	420,740	57.9
4.6	968	99.90	1.6	460,172	54.0
4.5	1,350	99.87	1.5	500,000	50.0
4.4	1,866	99.81	1.4	539,828	46.0
4.3	2,555	99.74	1.3	579,260	42.1
4.2	3,467	99.65	1.2	617,911	38.2
4.1	4,661	99.53	1.1	655,422	34.5
4.0	6,210	99.38	1.0	691,462	30.9
3.9	8,198	99.18	0.9	725,747	27.4
3.8	10,724	98.9	0.8	758,036	24.2
3.7	13,903	98.6	0.7	788,145	21.2
3.6	17,864	98.2	0.6	815,940	18.4
3.5	22,750	97.7	0.5	841,234	15.9
3.4	28,716	97.1	0.4	864,334	13.6
3.3	35,930	96.4	0.3	884,930	11.5
3.2	44,565	95.5	0.2	903,199	9.7
3.1	54,799	94.5	0.1	919,243	8.1

The values in this table reflect the 15 Sigma shift in the centering of a process that typically occurs over time.

Tree Diagram (continued)
Construction Steps:

1. Identify the goal statement the team is to accomplish.
2. Identify the next (first) level sub-goals, by answering the question, "How will I achieve that goal?"
3. Repeat the question "How will I..." for each of the sub-goals.
4. Continue to breakdown to the third or fourth level sub-goals.

Intro
Ready ?
6 Months
Project
Long Haul
DMAIIC
Tools
R&R

Click on any tool name in the following lists to get more information in the e-book.

Some abbreviations as needed:
C/S= Check Sheet
C/L= Check List
ROR=Rate of Return
W/S=Worksheet

Quick Links to the Tools of DMAIIC

Tool	D	M	A	I	I	C
Action Plan W/S				•		
Affinity Diagram	•	•	•	•		
Benchmarking	•			•	•	
Brainstorming	•		•	•		
CAPDo						•
Cause & Effect			•			
Change Mgmt. C/L					•	
Check Sheet		•	•	•	•	
Contingency Planning (PDPC)	•			•	•	
Contingency Table Analysis		•				
Control Charts	•	•	•	•		•
Cost-Benefit Anal./Future ROR				•	•	
Cost Factors C/L	•					
Countermeasures Eval. C/S			•			
Creativity Methods			•			
Critical Pathway Analysis (AND)			•			
Customer Interview Guide	•					
Customer Prioritization Table	•					
Customer Requirements Table	•			•		
Cycle Time Analysis	•	•		•		
DMAIIC Story						•
Design of Exp.		•	•			
Failure Mode & Effects Analysis		•	•	•		
Failure-to-Follow Analysis			•			
Flow Chart/Process Map	•		•	•		•
Force Field Analysis	•					
Gage R&R Study	•	•	•	•		
GANTT Chart	•					
Histogram		•	•	•		•
Implementation Training Matrix			•			

Tool	D	M	A	I	I	C
Interrelationship Digraph				•	•	
Layout Diagrams		•				•
Meeting Agenda	•					
Nominal Group Tech.	•					
Pareto Chart	•	•	•	•		
Prioritization Matrices					•	
Problem Statement Check List	•					
Process Book					•	•
Process Cap. Anal.	•	•	•	•		•
Process Deficiency Worksheet	•					
Process Inventory	•					
Process Mgmt. Charts		•			•	•
Process Profile	•		•			
Process Watch	•					
Project Charter Worksheet	•					
Project Launch Check List	•					
Project Plan - W/S	•			•		
Project Scorecard		•				•
Quality Function Deployment				•		
Responsibility Flow Chart	•	•		•		
Responsibility Matrix	•			•		
Run Chart		•	•	•	•	•
Scatter Diagram		•	•	•	•	
Six Sigma	•	•	•	•	•	•
Sigma Conv. Table	•					
Taguchi Methods			•			
Team Charter	•					
The 5 S's			•			
Tree Diagram	•			•	•	
Twenty Questions		•				
5 Whys			•			

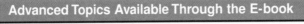

Advanced Topics Available Through the E-book

ANOVA, Analysis of Variance
Balanced Scorecard
Changing the Process
- Generate/Select Countermeasures
- Implement/Evaluate Results
- Standardize/Replicate Improvements
- Financial Analysis of Changes

Control Charts, Additional Topics
- Managing with Control Charts
- Control Charts for Sporadic Events
- Non-Normal Data and X, mR Charts
- Control Charts and ANOM
- CUSUM Control Chart, Detecting Small Average Shifts
- Short Run Control Charts
- Auto-Correlated Data on Control Charts
- Variable Limits for X-bar, R Control Charts

Correlation Analysis, Correlation Coefficient
Customer Research Methods
Data Collection
Data Displays:
- Understanding Variation
- Measures of Central Tendency & Variability
- Skewness and Kurtosis
- Frequency Chart

Detecting Differences
- Foundations of Probability and Statistics
- Hypothesis Testing
- Sampling Theory
- Statistics
- Distributions (Binomial, Poisson, Normal, Log Normal, Exponential, Weibull, Normal Distribution for Sampling Means, t-distribution, Chi-square, F-Distribution)

Intro

Ready ?

6 Months

Project

Long Haul

DMAIC

Tools

R & R

Intro

Ready ?

6 Months

Project

Long Haul

DMAIIC

Tools

R & R

Advanced Topics Available Through the E-book *(cont.)*

Design Management
- Defining Product/Service Requirements
- Conceptual Design
- Benchmarking
- Taguchi Design Approach

Experimentation (One factor, Multi-factor, Orthogonal Arrays)

Hypothesis Test: Means, Variation, Proportions

Measurement System Analysis
- Measure Error

Operating Reviews

Performance Indicators

Process Management
- Process Thinking
- Process Management Methods

Production Management, Lean Manufacturing

Regression Analysis, Linear Regressions

Reliability Management
- Reliability Concepts and Management
- Fault Tree Analysis
- Quantifying Reliability
- Root Cause Analysis

Sampling

Stratification
- Bar Charts
- Pie Charts

Team Facilitation & Management
- Working with Teams (teams, team processes)
- Idea Generation & Decision Making
- Conflict and other Team Wonders

Intro

Ready ?

6 Months

Project

Long Haul

DMAIIC

Tools

R & R

Chapter 8:
References & Resources

***Other places to learn about the "art" and "science" of
implementing Six Sigma***

Purpose of this chapter:

There are MANY outstanding resources available that support
the successful implementation of Six Sigma. This chapter high-
lights just a few of those resources that we have found to be
most helpful. These references are not intended as exclusive
endorsements of these resources. Others are referenced throughout the book and e-book.

Books

Change Management

Kotter, J. *Leading Change*. Cambridge, MA: Harvard Business
School Press, 1996.

Design of Experiments

Anderson, M, and Whitcomb, P. *DOE Simplified: Practical
Tools for Effective Experimentation*. Portland, OR: Productivity,
Inc., 2000.

Montgomery, D. *Design and Analysis of Experiments*. 5th ed.
New York: John Wiley & Sons, 2000.

Leadership

Kaplan, R., and Norton, D. *The Balanced Scorecard:
Translating Strategy into Action*. Boston, MA: Harvard
Business School Press, 1996.

Problem Solving

Brassard, M. *The Memory Jogger Plus: featuring the Seven
Management and Planning Tools*. Salem, NH: GOAL/QPC,
1996.

Brassard, M., Ritter, D., et al. *The Problem Solving Memory
Jogger*. Salem: NH: GOAL/QPC, 2000.

Project Management

Guide to the Project Management Body of Knowledge (PMBOK). Philadelphia, PA: Project Management Institute, 2000.

Martin, P. & Tate, K. *The Project Management Memory Jogger.* Salem, NH: GOAL/QPC, 1997.

Quality Systems and Methods

Juran, J. Editor. *Juran's Quality Control Handbook*. 4th ed. New York: McGraw-Hill, 1988.

Peach, R. Editor. *The ISO 9000 Handbook*. 3rd ed. New York: McGraw-Hill, 1996.

Peach, R., Peach, B., Ritter, D. *The Memory Jogger 9000/2000: A Pocket Guide to Implementing the ISO 9001 Quality Systems Standard Based on BSR/ISO/ASQ Q9001-2000.* Salem, NH: GOAL/QPC, 2000.

SPC

Amsden, R., Butler, H., Amsden, D. *SPC Simplified: Practical Steps to Quality.* 2nd ed. New York: Quality Resources, 1998. Also, *SPC Simplified For Services: Practical Tools for continuous Quality Improvement*, 1991.

Brassard, M. & Ritter, D. *The Memory Jogger II: A Pocket Guide of Tools for Quality.* Salem, NH: GOAL/QPC, 1994.

Grant, E., & Leavenworth, R. *Statistical Quality Control.* 7th ed. New York: McGraw-Hill, 1996.

Wheeler, D. & Chambers, D. *Understanding Statistical Process Control.* Knoxville, TN: SPC Press, 1992.

Teams

Scholtes, P., Joiner, B., Streibel, B. *The Team Handbook.* 2nd ed. Madison, WI: Oriel, Inc, 1996.

Web Sites

www.isixsigma.com - Frequently updated site featuring best practices, news, services and tools in support of 6 Sigma.

www.sixsigmaforum.com - Site established in 2001 by ASQ. Resources are customized to meet the needs of all Six Sigma "roles" - from Green Belt to the Executive.

www.premierperformance.net - Site of Premier Performance Network (PPN), pioneers in organization-wide quality management systems, including 6 Sigma, since the early 1980's. PPN's implementation model and materials provided the foundation for this book.

www.sixsigmabenchmarking.com - Site that's designed to provide a network for organizations implementing 6 Sigma. The site also includes pages for industry - and process specific benchmarking associations.

www.isssp.org - Site established by the International Society of Six Sigma Professionals to support specialists in the Six Sigma process.

www.superfactory.com - Site dedicated to electronically linking manufacturing excellence resources around the world. Check out their wide selection of "Virtual Factory Tours" to learn about manufacturing excellence or to satisfy your "how-do-they-make-that?" curiosity.

www.change-management.com - A change management resource site providing articles, books, tutorials, training, and benchmarking studies.

Organizations

American Society for Quality (ASQ), www.asq.org.

American Statistical Association (ASA), www.amstat.org.

Association for Manufacturing Excellence (AME), www.ame.org.

Association for Quality and Participation (AQP), www.aqp.org.

American Productivity and Quality Center (APQC), www.apqc.org.

National Institute of Standards and Technology/Baldrige National Quality Program, www.quality.nist.gov.

Project Management Institute (PMI), www.pmi.org.

Intro

Ready ?

6 Months

Project

Long Haul

DMAIIC

Tools

R & R

Intro

Ready ?

6 Months

Project

Long Haul

DMAIIC

Tools

R & R

Journals

The American Statistician – Quarterly publication of the American Statistical Association focusing on the application and teaching of statistical methods. ASA also publishes the *Journal of the American Statistical Association*, containing statistical theory and research, along with a number of journals dedicated to the needs of specific disciplines and industries.

Journal for Quality and Participation – AQP's Journal is published monthly.

Project Management Journal – Quarterly publication of the Project Management Institute.

Quality Digest – Monthly publication some general-interest quality articles with strong coverage of the technical and equipment aspects of quality, www.qualitydigest.com.

Quality Magazine – A monthly publication focused exclusively on quality assurance and process improvement in manufacturing, with a special emphasis on practical applications of metrology methods and statistical analysis, http://www.qualitymag.com.

Quality Progress – ASQ's monthly journal which include diverse articles on the technical and organization issues involved in the continuous improvement of quality and profits. ASQ also publishes journals dedicated to quality management, technology and engineering, as well as software quality. ASQ recently initiated a new publication, *Six Sigma Forum Magazine*, during 2001.

Target – A quarterly publication by the Association for Manufacturing Excellence focusing on a wide range of manufacturing innovations with the greatest emphasis placed on lean manufacturing and Kaizen activity.

Free Electronic Resources

APQC CenterView **monthly newsletter** – APQC, www.apqc.org/free, also publishes monthly electronic newsletters focusing on customer relationships, knowledge management and organizational effectiveness.

AQP Inbox – Monthly newsletter that covers the latest news about AQP, www.aqp.org/pages/inbox, quality & participation, and overall business excellence.

InsideQuality – A daily quality news site from Quality Digest, www.insidequality.com, that includes an "Ask the Expert" discussion-group feature that's moderated by leading authors in each topic area, including Six Sigma.

NIST/MBNQA – A wide variety of quality improvement case studies and "Issue Sheets" are available, www.quality.nist.gov.

Quality America – QA, www.qualityamerica.com/six_sigma.html, makes a wide variety of excellent full-text articles available on its site.

Quality eLine – A monthly newsletter from PQ Systems, www.pqsystems.com/qualityelinesubscribe.htm, which offers statistical help, technical tips, book reviews, new product information, and references to other useful web sites.

Quality Magazine – *Quality,* www.qualitymag.com, makes a wide variety of excellent full-text articles available on its site across 10 manufacturing topic areas. The site also features a monthly e-newsletter.

***Stat-Teaser* quarterly newsletter and *DOE FAQ Alert* monthly bulletin** – Very informative, practitioner-friendly electronic publications of StatEase, Inc., www.statease.com.

Intro

Ready ?

6 Months

Project

Long Haul

DMAIC

Tools

R & R

Index

Intro

Ready ?

6 Months

Project

Long Haul

DMAIIC

Tools

R & R

Intro
Ready ?
6 Months
Project
Long Haul
DMAIIC
Tools
R & R

Intro

Ready ?

6 Months

Project

Long Haul

DMAIIC

Tools

R & R